Camouflage

Passions erupt where boundaries break

A Novella

ANGELINA AMOSS

US English has been used throughout.

This is a work of fiction. Names, characters, businesses, places, events and incidents either are the products of the author's imagination or used in a fictitious manner. Any resemblance to actual persons, living or dead, or actual events is purely coincidental.

Camouflage Copyright © Angelina Amoss 2023 – All rights reserved

The rights of Angelina Amoss to be identified as the author of this work has been asserted by her in accordance with the Copyright, Designs & Patents Act 1988

No part of this book may be reproduced, or stored in a retrieval system, or transmitted in any form or by any means, electronic, mechanical, photocopying, recording, or otherwise, without the express written permission of the author. Quotes from the book may be used in reviews.

First Printed Edition, England April 2023

ISBN: 9798392086290

Book cover from Bookcoverzone.com

Index

Index	3
Book Description	4
With Thanks	5
The Fall	6
Nonsensical Attraction	14
Jettisoned	23
One Last Hurrah!	32
Point of no Return	36
Aladdin's Cave	40
Dancing in the Garden of Love	47
Truly, Madly, Deeply	56
Scorpion	62
Aspects of Love	69
Jealousy	81
Forbidden Fruit	88
Love Me	92
The Holiday	102
Armageddon	118
Swan-Song	131
Life after Love	145
Author Information	153

Book Description

CAMOUFLAGE – ANGELINA AMOSS

Life can be full of surprises.

Rose is a small-town wife, the epitome of respectability and stability, and the nucleus of her family. When she embarks on an affair at the age of sixty-three, she's completely shocked... succumbing to temptation goes against everything she believes in. Yet she's also excited and given an unexpected injection of life.

Joe is thirty-five, a happy-go-lucky, guitar-playing divorcé with a son he loves deeply. He's been searching for a meaningful relationship to complete his otherwise happy life. Deep and thoughtful, he is not normally a person who takes risks.

Rose and Joe have too much to drink at a party. Maybe it was that, or maybe it was something else. But, when Joe wraps his arms around her waist to dance with her, Rose's life begins to spin out of control.

It wasn't deliberate, but somehow forbidden love finds her. Passion erupts when she breaks boundaries, igniting within her desires long since dried up and lost. United in a beautiful yet haunting discovery, Joe and Rose will question everything, including loyalty.

***Camouflage** is an exploration of the complexities of relationships, and reflects on the many aspects of love and the choices we make in its pursuit.*

For fans of The Bridges of Madison County & Lady Chatterley's Lover.

With Thanks

My thanks go to Nigel, without his help this book would be dotted with errors. Thanks Nigel, for your editing and for being such a good friend.

Thank you to Dawn & Helen for being such good friends and great Beta readers, I appreciate your help and comments very much. Thanks also to Julie, a true friend whose encouragement keeps me going.

The Fall

Joe's arm is hugging my waist and out of nowhere, I realize I miss sex. He isn't being over-familiar. His hold is much more a 'let me hug my mum' kind of embrace. At first glance you might say it's rather sweet. But my jokingly 'adopted son' is having a crazy effect on me. His grip on my waistline is firm, very possessive. A flame of long-lost desire erupts inside me; it's shocking in its voracity. Get a grip, I urge my crazy emotions. It doesn't help. My thoughts and the core of my being are erupting with a million buried dreams and desires.

A quick search and my eyes find him, Harvey – the love of my life, standing in a group of men; laughing, eyes sparkling, enjoying the comradeship of talking football, politics, and most importantly dropping his dry, quick wit into every crack in the chatter.

Has he noticed Joe's hold on me? Would he care if he had?

Today is our ruby wedding anniversary – a joyous day when we celebrate the fact that we have put up with each up for forty years. We're blessed. Time has on the whole been kind. Through happy and sad occasions we have stood side-by-side, the two pillars of our loving family. I've never strayed, nor even been tempted in all our years together. I love my husband – that's not in question.

The question is... what's going on with me?

Right now, I want nothing more than to be whisked away by this young man. Am I crazy? Have I lost all sense?

Joe's hand slips from my waist and drops into my hand. Is it a statement? Just half an hour ago, I was telling everyone how Jake (our eldest child and Joe's best friend) always held my hand in public. He never cared what other kids thought. And here's Joe, not letting me go. Laughing about being Jake's adopted brother and therefore by default making me his adopted mother.

Why am I suddenly wishing I was young again?

I've always treated Joe like one of my kids, caring for him like a second mother. But I don't feel maternal right now – too much rum I guess. At this moment, I would like the world to disappear so I can stay here, in Joe's arms, enjoying feeling like a woman for the first time in like forever.

'Your glass is empty.' Luke, our other son, takes my glass from me with a smile. A shift of my feet and I step away from the man causing my turmoil. I should protest and say I've had enough to drink. Goodness knows when I last had this amount. I'd forgotten how alcohol numbs clarity of thought... and how my inhibitions dissolve. How brave I become! Brave enough to let my true self fly free. I'm currently enjoying being a kite, soaring through the night, adrift from the string that normality anchors me to... to... conventionality I guess.

Why has Joe suddenly become so attractive? Even if I was young, he wouldn't be my type. I like tall, chunky men.

I suck air in through my nose. Get a grip, get a grip!

But I don't want to be sensible. I want to step back and hold Joe's hand. As if I've secretly summoned him, he takes a step and closes the gap between us again, wrapping an arm around my shoulder. I want to turn my body so I can bury my face in his jumper. How ridiculous!

'Thanks.' I smile at Luke, accepting my rum and coke. I hope he hasn't made it too strong.

'How's life treating you, Mrs. Delaney?' asks Lucas, one of Luke's friends.

'Oh, you know – same old, same old. Nothing much changes once you retire.'

'Luke tells us you're writing a book.'

'Well, trying to write is probably more accurate.'

Did I just imagine it, or did Joe's grip around my shoulder just tighten? His warm breath trickles down my neck... it's heady, as is his aftershave. Damn, but musky cologne does something for me!

'Happy anniversary Mrs. Delaney,' says Mary, a friend of our daughter Gemma.

I'm suddenly acutely aware of just how many of our children's friends are here. They've always come to our parties; they're like an extension of our family. Only now I'm aware that they're no longer children. When did they grow up?

A roar of laughter from the other side of the room draws my eyes back to my hubby. Surrounded by his male friends he's in his element and in cracking form. How far away he seems to me right now, almost a stranger. Where have the last forty years gone? We didn't start off with this distance between us.

Chasing Cars comes on. 'I love this song.' I thought I had said it in my head, but I guess not, because Joe is pulling me out of the crowd to an area we had cleared for dancing. I feel like I'm sleepwalking. How much have I had to drink? I don't care that Joe is holding me way too close. It's hard to think. His hand feels soft yet firm, his grip is nice.

I sniff his neck and then freeze in the act. What am I doing?

I try to put a few inches between our bodies. I wobble. 'Don't let me fall.'

He grabs my arm and pulls me back to his body. 'I've got you, Rose.'

Oh flipping rhubarb sticks! He's got me!

Move... I've got to move. 'Hey, Ian,' I call to my husband's best friend. 'You like to waltz, don't you? Come on let's have a dance.'

He flies to my rescue, his drunken body swaying in delight as he whisks me out of Joe's arms. We stumble around for about eight steps and then I have to call a halt before we crash to the floor.

'Thanks Ian.' I kiss his cheek and beeline for the garden. I need fresh air.

It's been a lovely sunny June day, but the evening is cool. To keep warm, guests are gathered around three chimineas spaced around the patio, huddled in groups: talking, drinking, and laughing. So absurdly normal. This is a party like hundreds we've had before, and yet it isn't. Something has shifted.

'Hey,' calls Melody, 'where you been hiding?'

'I've not been hiding.' Good gracious, I've not been hiding have I?

'We were just talking about you,' says Darla.

'Oh no, what have I done now?'

My three friends laugh. 'Nothing yet,' confirms Daphne. 'We were just discussing a girlie retreat, maybe at the Lakes, are you up for it?'

Up for it? Goodness yes, I'm up for *anything* right now it seems. 'Sure,' I smile. 'When are you thinking of going?'

'Towards the end of the month, let's get together for lunch during the week and make plans,' Melody grins.

'Sounds good.' Maybe a break is what I need? I certainly need something because my pants are on fire and I think I need a shower.

The girls are in jolly form and the banter between them bounces, I smile and nod, I hope at the right places. I'm here, standing with my friends, but my head is somewhere else entirely. All I can think about is Joe's arm around my waist. I shiver.

I must look cold, because suddenly Joe is in front of me, offering me his leather jacket. Where did he come from? Slightly puzzled I slip my arms into the sleeves as he puts it on me.

'I can't remember the last time a guy gave me his coat,' I tell him.

He grins.

I look at the floor. I'm searching for something but I can't put my finger on it. 'I must have been about twenty,' I tell him finally looking up again. 'It makes me feel… it makes me feel…' Lordy how much have I had to drink? I can't even describe how it makes me feel. 'I guess it makes me feel like I'm twenty again.'

Tomorrow, I will remember what my rum-addled brain is searching for, the word to describe how I feel – protected. It's a blooming good job I don't recall it until tomorrow because everyone is looking at me.

'Ha!' I cry. 'Time to dance!' I take off the jacket given to me only moments before, put it on the back of a garden chair and rush inside to hit the floor and make some moves. Yes, sixty-three-year-olds still like to dance! Just please don't watch us too closely.

Ian is with me in a moment, quick-step or waltz or alcohol-induced muddled steps; who knows? We laugh our way around the small area left clear to shake our booties. His hand is in the small of my back, he squeezes my hand with his other. Oh sweet Ian, I know you'd like to whisk me away, and if life was different who knows I might let you.

'My turn.' Harvey whisks me out of Ian's arms. I wrap my arms around his neck and we sway. This is our song, *Volare* by *Dean Martin*, the one we danced to at our wedding forty years ago today. I'm only half aware that people have formed a circle around us and are singing, as are we, along with Dean. Our bodies are welded together, we smile lovingly into each other's eyes; people can tell that after all these years we still love each other enormously. 'Volare oh oh, E cantare, oh oh oh oh…' *(Dean Martin 1989)*

An hour later, I'm in the bathroom.

Why do I feel like crying?

I love that I am old enough to be a granny. My grandchildren bring me so much joy. I've never minded getting old before…

…Before Joe put his arm around my waist, and without realizing it awoke the dormant *woman* inside me.

I wrap my arms around my body and close my eyes. I imagine Joe nuzzling my neck. His kiss would be warm and soft.

'Stupid woman!' I scrub my hands like they're covered in ink.

Three deep breaths, double-check my make-up hasn't smudged, and then I head back to the party.

Why do I feel like crying? Maybe it's because my hubby never wraps his arms around me in quite the same way that Joe just did. Maybe it's because Joe's touch awoke a yearning within me that has been gone for a long time. A time when young blokes chatted me up and found me attractive.

Aging is shitty. It's good too sometimes, but mostly it's just shitty.

Is it time's fault or mine that I have let myself go? I'm the one who overeats and doesn't apply face cream every day. I'm the one who prefers the car to walking and the downstairs loo to the stairs. Maybe it's not time's fault that I look in the mirror and hate myself. I was a right plain Jane before aging. Now I'm just *ugh!*

How could I possibly think that a young man would find me attractive? Any man for that matter!

If he was a bit too close to me, surely it was just his beer goggles misguiding him? I would do well to suggest he visit the opticians tomorrow rather than return his hugs.

For the rest of the party I try to behave like the sixty-three-year-old that I am. But damn that club music, because its thud-thud lulls me into forgetting... age, time, crumbling discs, arthritic knees. All the elements of age disappear as my body syncs with the beat. I hear Jake laughing and look up to find him in front of me, arms in air, dancing his heart out. In moments, Luke and Gemma are with us. My children have inherited my love of club music. We pound the floor and wave our arms, could life get any better?

It's three in the morning, the last of our guests are leaving. I have been avoiding him, but here he is to say goodnight.

But he doesn't *say* anything. He just looks into my eyes until my heart is beating so hard I think my head will explode. His arms slide around me. Firm. Possessive. His hold is a continuation of the stare and his unspoken yet clearly seen question... do you feel the same, Rose?

Nonsensical Attraction

SUNDAY HAS COME AND GONE and I've seen none of it. Well, not until seven-thirty in the evening when I finally pull myself out of bed and go downstairs.

'Here you go, love.'

I can't believe he's made me a bacon butty, part of me is starving for it, the other part is thankful I've not thrown up yet and I'm not sure I want to risk it now.

'You should eat, you'll feel better.'

'Thanks.'

I snuggle into the sofa and nibble the sandwich. He's right; it's restoring some life into me. He joins me shortly, with two cups of tea.

'You're my angel!'

He chuckles and gets comfy. He takes the control and switches over to a crime drama. I would have liked to carry on watching the nature program that was on, but I don't protest. I like some murder mysteries, not all of them though.

We sit in silence. It's comfortable. I'm glad he doesn't ask me if I had a good time or why I drank too much. I'm sure he's glad I don't ask him what he did in his study for an hour after I went to bed. Some things are just private.

ALL I CAN THINK OF IS JOE. I've spent five days obsessing about him. I'm gripped with the conviction that I'm stupid, but I just can't stop. I've had love songs on repeat on my YouTube channel and spent hours caught up in the fantasy of *what if*. Luckily, Harvey is enjoying a snooker week and has been in his den nearly all week. Today, as per normal for a Saturday, he's at the golf club. I skipped lunch with the girls; somehow I thought I might blurt out what's going on with me because they'd be sure to spot something. And I don't want to admit that anything's going on – to them or myself. They've picked a date to go away and called me to confirm. I cried off, making up excuses that I hope sounded genuine.

I'm in the process of making a cottage pie for dinner when there's a light tap on the door followed by a greeting, 'Hello?'

I freeze. What's Joe doing here? I turn around slowly as I hear him approach. He's been in the kitchen a million times before, but today his presence stirs up an atmosphere that's both sparkling with life and crushing impropriety.

'Jake's not here today.'

Why is my heart beating so fast?

'I came to see you.'

I badly want to swear, I keep my lips pinched closed.

'Can I pop the kettle on?'

I nod. He doesn't normally ask, this is his home-from-home, and he knows he's welcome. Change has occurred, everything is different. As Joe prepares two cups of tea, I go back to preparing dinner. I need to keep busy and stop my hands from shaking.

He brings the cups over to the counter where I'm chopping vegetables. He doesn't ask if I need (or want) help. He simply pulls open a drawer, selects another peeler and sets to work on the carrots. We peel, chop, and wash, the whole time he stands with his shoulder millimetres away from mine. When our hands brush against each other, electricity shoots up my arm. In silence we ask each other a thousand questions.

His presence is scaring me. He's like a panther waiting to pounce. The fact I want to be caught petrifies me. I sneak glances at him, hoping my hair will cover my studious glances. I've known him since he was five. Today he's a stranger... and a man, a person I've never seen before. I think I could lose myself in him, water to a sponge. My mind is filled with the stuff of young girls.

I'm sixty-three. I'm blooming sixty-three!

Why do I feel like a teenager?

We work in silence, I can hear my heart racing in my ears, its thud-thud is deafening. I go to mash the boiled potatoes. He takes the masher from me. His finger purposely traces over my hand. I catch my breath and look up at him. A three-second look and we tell each other we want something forbidden.

He puts the masher down and moves even closer to me. I should move away. Why can't I move?

He brushes the hair off my face. I feel sick. I close my eyes.

When his lips brush against mine, I moan. I take a step back. He puts his arms around me and pulls me back to him.

I should run. I should scream. I should push him away.

I melt into him. My breasts push against him as his arms hold me tight.

I'm lost.

My mind is trying to protest, but my body is responding in a way it shouldn't. I am alive. I am young. I am desired. I'm so wicked! I struggle a bit and finally release myself from him. I'm panting, and full of lust.

'You should go.'

'I don't want to.'

I can't help laughing. I don't want him to go either, but he must. I'm not this person. I don't cheat, I don't have affairs. I. Am. Not. This. Person.

'Go home, Joe.'

Uncertainty flickers across his eyes. I hate putting the light out in them but I must.

'Go.'

He nods his acceptance. Bends, kisses me on the cheek and leaves.

When the door shuts, I collapse on a chair. Oh my giddy aunt, what's going on? I lift a finger and touch my lips. They feel bruised and swollen. I wrap my arms around my body and sit. I think I'm in shock. It's a long time before I get up to finish making dinner.

I CRADLE MY CUP with both hands and stare into the garden. Years of tender care have gone into the borders, shrubs, and trees. It's my own little piece of Paradise. Both Harvey and I are rather proud of it. Over the years it has been my source of peace. Today, as I sit in the conservatory looking out my normal appreciation for it is missing.

I'm caught in a timeless struggle. Sixty-three years of playing by the rules and maintaining the height of propriety, sixty-three years of drummed-in regulations and boundaries are *strangling* me. That wall of respectability is crumbling. In doing so it's revealing the real me, hidden inside, longing to burst out. Pious sensibilities and callous assumptions (and prejudices) cause us to judge and cast aspersions over what we *see*, but we criticize the harshest when we judge ourselves.

A part of me is screaming that I'm the wickedest woman who ever lived. Another part is begging me to be adventurous, to pick up the phone and call him. I won't though. I can't. I touch my lips. The memory is delicious, my body responds in a startling way.

I stand up and walk over and lay my forehead against the cool glass.

What is wrong with me? Why do I feel like this?

My world is spinning.

I know we are nothing more than spoiled children if we chase after everything we want. Confessing to myself that I want Joe is not an easy thing. It's hard. It's painful. Yet I'm longing for his touch with such intensity it's frightening.

Another week has passed and I'm more consumed with thoughts of Joe every day.

Joe. Joe, are you thinking about me? Can you feel my soul calling to yours? Am I just crazy?

Joe. Joe, I can't stop thinking about you. Are you thinking about me? Did that kiss affect you the way it affected me? Probably not. Of course not! I'm just a crazy old woman!

Yet longing is building inside me. I know it's there, unfurling like a sleeping cat. I want to be touched... in that way. In the way that Joe touched me. I want to feel like a woman again. Be young again. Stupid old woman!

What do you think of me, Joe? Have you even given me a second thought in this last week? I hope you have, oh God I hope you have.

I'm finding it hard to concentrate on anything. The TV has become a blur of light and sound. Words in a book get up and dance around the page. In the last week – since the kiss, I've managed to only read three pages and even those I can't recall.

※ ❦ ※

SATURDAY IS HERE AGAIN – and so is Joe. He waited for me to answer the door this time. We don't speak, I open the door wide and he comes in and goes straight to the kitchen and puts the kettle on.

I've been calling to his soul, and here he is. I did this. Crazy old woman.

He's getting out the cups and tea things. His hands are shaking. A nervous energy pours from his lithe body – a body I'm longing to touch. I'm out of sorts. I sit on a chair and put my hands under me, as if to stop them reaching out to touch him. I watch his every move, devouring every bit of him with my eyes.

He brings over two cups of tea and sits down opposite me. We stare at each other over the kitchen table.

'Let's sit in the garden,' I say standing up and heading out.

He follows me and we sit at the table on the patio, under the shade of the blooming clematis. Its deep purple flowers are open and smother the pergola with their sweet aroma.

Joe takes out his tobacco tin. 'Do you mind?'

I shake my head. Harvey smokes, about ten a day, always in the garden though never in the house and always away from me. Unless we're out and then he's not so considerate, especially after a drink; he's made me cough numerous times over the years, I'm used to it now, though I've never smoked in my life.

I'm caught up with Joe's long, elegant fingers as he rolls his cigarette.

'Good guitar fingers,' he says catching my stare.

I wonder how explorative his fingers are. Then I wonder what the blooming heck is happening to me!

'I can't remember the last time I heard you play.'

'I've hardly picked up the guitar since Freddie was born, life gets a bit busy, as you know.'

'Oh, but you should. I used to love listening to you.'

No words come from his mouth, but his quick glance speaks volumes. I don't know how I know, but I sense he's about to start playing again.

After a short silence I say, 'You know *he* could have been home.'

'I checked for his car before I knocked.'

Clandestine... I never knew Joe was like that. 'What brings you here, Joe?' My longings? Yours?

'I wanted to see you.'

'Here I am.' I shrug, lift my hands up. Waiting for... I'm not a hundred percent sure what for. I'm just glad he's here.

'About last Saturday...'

I sip my tea. He's brave I'll give him that. I would never have brought it up. I would have buried it deep and let it die a slow, painful death. I watch him over the rim of my cup, holding it in front of me like a shield.

I see him falter, looking confused. I feel sorry for him but I don't speak.

'Freddie's going to be in the school play next week.'

He's backed off, changed his mind. I'm glad. Let's bury this sin before it consumes us.

'I've got two tickets to watch him. It's on Thursday at 5.30 pm. Will you come with me? Felicity's away again, so with his mum not able to come I think he'd appreciate his substitute Granma being there.'

I cringe.

Joe looks alarmed. 'Obviously, if you're busy…'

A hundred tiny daggers hit me when he said Granma and reminded me of my age. But I can't let him know that's the reason for the painful grimace. 'It's just I've done my share of school events.'

'Yes, of course, I understand. In a two-hour play, I'll only be awake for the ten minutes that Freddie's on stage.' His laugh is weak.

'Maybe you could both join us for dinner afterwards? You know Thursday nights are family meal time, so everyone will be here.' And that's when you should come, when everyone's here. Not when I'm home alone and longing to kiss you. It will be safe for you to come then, safer than now when my body wants to pounce.

'Sure, that'll be great, thanks.' He stands. He hasn't finished his tea.

My heart sinks. I want to be bad. I want to kiss again.

I walk him to the door; it's not something I've done before.

He turns and engulfs me in a hug. It's tight. It's also much longer than a hug should be. It seems neither of us wants to let go. Finally, he pulls away, only to lock eyes with me.

What's he saying? I want to know. What are my eyes saying? Do they give me away?

He goes. I shut the door and then lean back against it. What's happening between us? Why do I feel so giddy?

Jettisoned

I'VE NOT SEEN JOE FOR TWO WEEKS. I miss him. I'm longing for him, yearning for the feel of his lips on mine. I've spring-cleaned the entire house, emptying cupboards that haven't seen the light of day for years. It's burning up my excess energy physically – but mentally I'm a mess!

I wish I'd gone away with the girls now, it would have been fun.

I decide to call Gemma. I'm going to ask her to come out to lunch with me, maybe do some mother-daughter window shopping. We haven't done that in ages. I want someone to talk to.

'Hi love, how's it going?'

'Oh mum, I was just going to ring you.'

'You were?'

'Yes. Harry's got a cold and the crèche won't take him in. I was planning to meet Mary today, she's got us a morning spa pass and I was looking forward to just unwinding and switching off for a bit. You wouldn't mind having Harry for a few hours, would you?'

I want adult conversation. I want to go for lunch with my daughter and have a catch-up. I wants don't get – I used to tell my kids. 'Of course I can. I'll be with you in twenty minutes.'

'Oh thanks Mum, you're a life-saver.'

'See you soon.'

Last month I would have been overjoyed to look after Harry, pleased that my daughter could switch off and enjoy herself for a while. I remember how hard it was bringing up three young children. Today is a different matter. Today I feel used and taken for granted, surly even.

What is happening to me?

I have a childish moment. I don't rush. I look around the house making sure there isn't anything I should do before I go, so I can make myself late. There's nothing. The house is so clean you could eat your dinner off the floor. I pick up my book, *The Bridges of Madison County*, and put it in my bag just in case Harry has a nap. I saw the film years ago. The short love affair between *Clint Eastwood* and *Meryl Streep* made me cry. I'd wanted her to leave her husband and chase happiness.

Gemma and Ethan only live ten minutes away from us by car. I was over the moon when they first bought the house, delighted that my daughter wanted to live close to me. Now I wonder if it was just so they had a babysitter on tap. That thought rocks me and makes me hate myself. I'm more to them than that, I know I am. We're a loving family, very close. I hate this new me, I want the old me back. Tears sting my eyes.

I dab at my face before getting out of the car. I don't want Gemma to see the mess I'm in.

'Hi love,' I call as I walk in.

Gemma comes into the hallway, a large smile on her beautiful face. I'm filled with remorse for thinking negative thoughts about her. We hug. I hold her extra hard and longer than normal.

'You OK, Mum?'

I smile. 'Yes of course. Now, where's my little angel?'

'In his bouncy chair in front of the TV, *Teletubbies* is the only thing that soothes him right now.'

'Poor love.'

'If it's OK I'm going to scoot right away? Mary's waiting for me to pick her up.'

'That's fine.'

'You sure you're OK Mum?'

'Absolutely.'

She hovers, a worried frown on her face. Her lips move like she's going to say something. In the end, she decides to drop it. She gives me a brief hug, picks up her bag and with a last smile leaves me alone with my grandson.

'Hello sweetheart,' I say bending down to kiss Harry on the head. On seeing my face, his arms spring up inviting me to pick him up. My cup overflows. I love him so much. I love all my grandchildren. All of them perfect in their own little way. He snuggles backward until he's comfy on my lap and sucks his thumb. I sigh. How innocent are the young. No wickedness flowing through their veins.

Harry coughs and sniffles and fidgets on my lap, until eventually, after half a bottle of milk, he falls asleep. I don't want to put him upstairs on his own, so I make him a bed on the sofa and cover him up, keeping him close to me so that I can keep my hand stroking his forehead whenever he moans. Sweet little angel.

I switch off the telly and pull the book out of my bag. I've started it already. I never realized when I watched the film that it was a true story; somehow that fact makes it all the more poignant. Reading how *Robert Waller* was approached by the children of Francesca to write the book brings a lump to my throat. I thought I wouldn't cry because I already know the story, but knowing part of the story (the film) doesn't prepare me for all the intricate details that Francesca left in her diaries.

As I read, tears stream down my cheeks. I'm just as sad for myself as I am for Francesca and Kincaid.

I'M TRYING TO BE A GOOD PERSON. I'm in giving mode big style. My time and energy are being poured into my family. I want everyone to be happy. This morning, when I couldn't sleep, I got up at 5 am and made Chelsea buns. The process is long, time-consuming and requires my patience. The house smells like a bakery, it's heavenly.

'Can't remember the last time you made Chelsea buns.'

I grin as Harvey comes in and sits at the kitchen table. Maybe he'll spend the day with me today. 'I haven't made them since Jake left home.'

'What made you do them today? Not that I'm complaining... I love them!'

'I thought I would drive around to all the kids and drop them off a batch each.'

'Arr, an excuse to see them.'

'I don't need an excuse to see my children!'

'No, of course not, I was just teasing.'

I make a pot of tea, and we sit and eat some buns while doing a crossword together. I like our morning puzzles, hopefully they will help keep our minds sharp.

When we've finished two buns each, a pot of tea and three puzzles – and before he leaves for his den, I ask, 'I was thinking about going out for a walk. Would you like to come with me? I know it's not sunny, but it's not raining and it'll be fresh. I thought we could go to the reservoir.'

'Sorry Rose, I've got a game booked with Ian this morning.'

Golf, always flipping golf!

'It's Friday!' Sometimes I hate golf for stealing my husband away from me.

'I know, but we're practicing before the match tomorrow.'

I guess if he was in the house all the time that would drive me crazy. 'No worries, I'm quite content to go on my own.' I kiss him on the head and he gives me a broad smile. Once upon a time his smile used to melt my heart.

Walking shoes on and a cardigan tied around my waist I set off. I don't want to drive to the reservoir on my own. It's a bit isolated. The last time I went, I got a cold sensation on my neck as if someone might be following me. Better to stay here and just walk along the canal like I usually do.

※ ❤ ※

'HI LOVE, WHAT BRINGS YOU HERE?' Jake isn't smiling, something is wrong. 'What's happened?'

The one thing a mother wants is for her kids to be happy. She can only be happy knowing they are well and happy. Anything that goes wrong in their lives has a direct effect on her. My stomach sinks.

'Penny's cheated on me.' The words are choked and he starts to sob.

'Oh love.' I'm by his side in a heartbeat, wrapping my arms around him tightly, hushing in his ear and stroking his hair. 'I'm so sorry, sweetheart, so sorry.'

I let him cry it out and when he pulls away to get a tissue, I take the opportunity to switch the kettle on.

'Thanks,' he says taking the cup and sitting down at the table.

'Do you want to tell me what happened?'

'She cheated on me.'

'Yes you said that, I mean the details?' I'm sad because I like Penny rather a lot and I'd hoped the two of them would end up together permanently.

'She said it was an accident.'

Aren't they always? I reach over and take his hand but keep my thoughts to myself. I could smack her right now for hurting my son.

'They went on a works bonding weekend.'

'Yes I remember her telling me they were going, a whole weekend away in a posh hotel all paid for by work.'

'Including alcohol apparently, and you know she doesn't normally drink that much.'

Oh my goodness, he wants to forgive her! My heartbeat quickens, I don't know how I feel about that. 'Just an occasional glass of wine isn't it?'

'Yeah, only two glasses, because she doesn't like how it makes her feel.'

Oh no, oh no, he's going to forgive her, he's making excuses for her already and he hasn't even given me the details yet. I don't want him to forgive her. *I* won't be able to forgive her for hurting my baby boy.

'So, she had too much to drink and ended up in someone else's bedroom?'

'That's the long and short of it. She said as soon as it happened she knew she'd made a terrible mistake and broke down. She told me all about it as soon as she came home, despite her friends telling her not to. She said she couldn't live with a lie between us.' Jake starts sobbing again.

How very noble! And what utter rubbish! Most people live with lies between them, if they didn't everyone would be divorced. I would have preferred her confession had been given to God and his forgiveness sought. That way Jake wouldn't be hurting right now. I could throttle her!

I move my chair next to his and pull him in for a hug. 'Poor love!'

After a while he goes to the bathroom to wash his face with cold water. I pour tea from the teapot and refill our cups.

'What should I do, Mum?' he asks when he comes back.

Leave her – run a hundred thousand miles away from her. 'That's a decision only you can make, Jake.' Please leave her.

'I don't know what to do. I love her. I don't think I can live without her.'

Sigh! The rubbish we tell ourselves. 'Of course you could live without her.'

'You think I should break up with her?'

'You haven't already?'

'No. I told her I needed some space. I was thinking I could come home for a while.'

'That's a good idea. Put a bit of distance between you. Give you both some time to reflect.' Hopefully enough time to realize you deserve better than a cheat.

'Thanks, Mum. Is Dad home?'

Is he ever? 'Not at the moment, but he'll be home for tea. Why don't you go and pack a bag and then come home?'

'I've already got a bag in the boot.'

'Well there you go then. Go and unpack, I'll do us some lunch. I've got some homemade butternut squash soup we can have.'

'Fab, I love your soups. What we having for dinner?'

'It's Friday, so it's steak and chips like always. You know your father won't have anything else on Fridays.' Even though I'm not a great meat eater.

'Does Dad know how lucky he is?' He gives me a hug, and I hug him back. My hurting grown-up baby. I wish I could take his pain away. He sighs. 'You're the best, Mum.'

'Go on with you, go and unpack.'

It warms my heart that my children still need me, for whatever reason. I'm glad they want to turn to me and that they include me in their lives. But just once, every now and again, I'd love them to come and visit me to simply ask, 'How you doing, Mum?'

JAKE MADE PENNY CRY EVERY DAY for a week, and then went back to her. It's what he wants, and who am I to argue? I pretend I'm happy with it, but I'm not, I'm *really* not. They've only been together for two years and she's cheated already. I don't think it bodes well for the future, I hope I'm wrong.

It's not lost on me that I'm being hypocritical, quick to condemn one who has transgressed, while I spend every moment of my waking life daydreaming of Joe.

I don't know where he's gone, but he seems to have slipped away from our lives altogether. It's for the best, but it hasn't stopped me longing for him. Every time someone is at the door I hold my breath hoping it's him. Disappointment is now my constant companion. I told him to go, and he did, I love that about him, that he'll do what I ask even when it's not what he wants to do. It's respectful.

My thoughts on the other hand are anything but respectful! They're downright scandalous. It's been five weeks now since I last saw Joe, but my desire for him hasn't faded. My fantasies are skyrocketing. I don't know who I am anymore.

One Last Hurrah!

STANDING IN THE BATHROOM gazing at the stranger reflected back at me, I shiver. I'm cold and in a thick fog. Everything is blurred and I'm confused.

I had been in a strange place being seduced. When a hand had run up the inside of my left thigh, I'd been alarmed at how real and dangerous it felt. I'm being pulled back into the world of comfortable shoes and dull clothes. This is where I belong. No lacy underwear or stockings. No danger. But boy, I'd been aroused and sexy in that place!

A voice is on repeat, drawing me into cold reality. 'Love, are you alright?'

Blink – a moment between dreams and waking.

Relieved air gushes from him when I finally come to. 'Come on, sweetheart. Let's get you back into bed. You've been sleepwalking again.'

I don't want to come back. The dream is slipping away and I'm experiencing loss.

'How did you know I was sleepwalking?' I ask as he pulls the covers over me.

'I heard you gasping; it gave me a shock at first.'

Gasping? How strong had that dream been?

'Try and get a bit more sleep, it's only five o'clock.' He kisses me on the forehead and leaves.

I hadn't been with Joe, that's surprising. I'd been with a stranger, one whose face remained hidden in shadow. He'd been rough, I instinctively know he would have hurt me, yet I'm in a state of loss because now he's gone.

Why didn't I dream of Joe?

I can't go back to sleep, my mind is in overdrive.

I hadn't realized that I'd been looking for something indefinable. I'd felt cocooned and safe in my skin. Now, I see that my body has a will of its own, yearning for connection it set about within me a subterfuge of restlessness and a terrifying desire for something more. Not knowing I was at war with my body, in the last few weeks, I had taken up walking on a grand scale. Punishing my feet and back, causing pain to consume the restlessness. Weight has fallen from my plump body and I've returned (with much glee) to clothes at the back of the wardrobe not worn for years.

My body, far from waving the white flag, has become more energetic, causing a fidgety nervous disposition within me. To compensate I've been punishing both my mind and body with excessive dull labor. Every cupboard and nook and cranny in the house has been emptied, cleaned and restocked with military precision. I did some online research and ended up offering my services to a church-run charity. Whether people are immobile or broke I don't ask or care, I simply like being a taxi for people who need lifts to hospital. I am busy. I am doing. But something inside me continues to scream for attention.

It seems the sensual side of me wants one last 'hurrah' before switching off. On the night of the party, like a sentient entity, my lust had reached through my flesh and revealed itself to Joe.

Joe of all people! I can't begin to explain the myriad of confusion that choice delivers. Funny how age becomes immaterial when you fall in love… or lust. In different lights

I alternatively see him as young and old. I wonder if it is the same for him.

I CAN'T BELIEVE I'M IN *Ann Summers!* I've managed to live sixty-three years and never been tempted inside, yet here I am. It was the mannequin that lured me in, well what it was displaying. Firstly, I appreciate that the mannequin is shaped like a voluptuous woman and not a skinny twig. Secondly, the black lacey bodice she's wearing seems both pretty and sexy.

I glance around the clothes rails.

'Good morning, would you like any help?' asks a beautiful and elegant shop assistant.

I can feel myself turning red. 'Umm, no thank you, I'm just looking.'

'Well just come over if you'd like some assistance.' She smiles and leaves me to my embarrassment. How times have changed! The shop isn't exactly packed, but there are lots of women in here, and quite a few men, like it's the most natural thing in the world to do – walking around a sex shop looking at toys in public. I have stepped into a new era.

I find the item that lulled me in. It's called *Starlet Crotchless Body.* I finger the material, it is super soft. I wonder what it would look like on me. I want to try it on, but I can't quite bring myself to lift it off the rail.

Convinced I'm too old for this stuff I rush out of the shop and head to Marks and Sparks.

Here I am comfortable, lots of women my age for a start! I want to laugh at myself for being such a prude. I've been walking around the shopping center for quite some time, and my back is telling me it's time to sit down but I've not found what I'm looking for so I grin and bear the pain.

At last, this is perfect. A push-up, underwired lacey bra with matching undies. Trust me – I need all the push-up I can get! I can't decide between the red and the black and in an uncommon moment of extravagance buy both sets.

When I get home I try them on and like what I see. In a rare moment of looking in the mirror and not hating my image, I stand and preen. Losing weight definitely suits me; I look much better when my double chin isn't so big, and the underwear, rather than make me cower with self-hate, looks good on me. I feel good, sexy even. I can't wait to wear them... although I have no idea when that will be.

I fold them carefully and place them in the bottom of my drawer. I discard the packaging under a pile of other rubbish and take it straight out for the bin making sure there is no chance it will be seen. I'm a frugal woman and seldom buy myself things, Harvey is always saying I should treat myself more, but I'm not sure he'd understand why I purchased today's items, to be honest I'm not even sure.

Point of no Return

I'M DEVOURING BOOKS, one after another, seeking sanctuary in the lives of made-up people. Laughing, crying, and sighing. Keeping my mind active and off Joe.

I have become the mistress of nonchalance, draping my camouflage around me with the precision and care of a florist creating a centerpiece of biblical proportions. See me! I am happy. I am content. I am a mother, wife, grandmother and friend. I am kind and thoughtful, considerate. I am *not* an adulteress… except maybe in my thoughts.

I've been in the library for about forty minutes. I can't decide on my next batch of books. I'm getting fed up with happy romances; they're making me bitter and jealous. With doom and gloom my current companions I pull *Wuthering Heights* off a shelf. I open the first page to see if it's something I will read. After ten pages, I'm still in the description of the place by Mr. Lockwood, I know the story is a classic but I'm not sure I will have the patience to read it at the moment. I'm about to take it to a chair and see if I can get into it, when someone covers my eyes with their hands.

'Guess who?'

The voice strikes a gong inside me and my body vibrates with the thrill of electricity, excitement, and life.

'Oh, I don't know – the librarian?'

Joe laughs and removes his hands.

Please touch me again. I turn around slowly. My heart is thudding like a blacksmith's hammer. I try to keep my grin under control. 'Hello Joe. How you doing?'

His sparkling eyes draw me in, they hold me captive. I'm content.

'I'm not doing so good as it happens.' He pulls a comical sad face.

'You're not?' Worry makes me blink several times. 'Is Freddie OK?'

'He's good.'

'But you're not?'

He shakes his head. 'I've tried to stay away from you, Rose, tried putting you out of my mind. Told myself a million times that I'm being crazy, that anything that might happen between us would just be crazy. Wrong.'

'But here you are.'

'It's a *public* library.'

'So you're looking for a book?'

'No. I'm looking for you. I saw you come in, I've been waiting for you to come out again, but you seem to never want to leave, so here I am.'

'Looking for me.'

'Finding you.'

It's so wrong. Everything about us is wrong. There should be no *us*. But there is, there most definitely is. 'What are you going to do now you've found me?' Where did that come from? Who spoke? Not me.

Before I can protest, Joe pulls me against him and starts kissing me. I kiss him back. My body is on fire. I lean into him. Don't let me go, Joe, don't let me go.

He pulls back, breathless. His pupils are fully dilated and deepest black. Joe, who over the years has appeared so aloof, is revealing the deep waters that run through him. My quiet, considerate Joe with his laughing eyes and quick humor, Joe, the boy who's become a man – a man who wants the woman in me.

'We should go somewhere else,' he says.

'Where?'

I think for a moment he is going to suggest his place. Instead he says, 'Let's grab a coffee.'

I think I'm more than a little disappointed, but I nod, and make my way to the exit. My books left discarded on an empty table.

In the car park we stop, once more our eyes lock. Oh chocolate heaven draw me in, don't let me go.

'Rose?' His voice is breathy, heavy. I guess he sees my need.

'Let's have coffee at your place.'

'Are you sure?'

'One hundred percent.'

He's hesitant. Does he not want me the way I want him? 'Or we can just go to the café.'

'My place is good.'

We nod at each other. An agreement made, a bridge crossed. We're slipping; the layers of conformity, masks, professionalism, all dissolving.

If you've ever experienced the one true love of your life, a love that for some reason could never be, you will understand why (married for forty years to my best friend) I'm about to stray. We are irrevocably drawn together, Joe and I. We know it's wrong. We know the fallout could be disastrous.

I'm about to risk everything in an endeavor to find my true self.

I am past the point of no return.

Aladdin's Cave

I'VE NOT BEEN IN JOE'S flat since the day he moved in. We helped him that day, when he was still sad from splitting up with Felicity. He'd been resigned, not to a single life, but to being a part-time dad, he hadn't been happy about that part of the divorce.

The mystery of an Aladdin's cave tickles the back of my neck. Being here is naughty, like I've sneaked into the pictures without paying. I wander around drinking in the tiny things that give away his character.

There's a painting on the wall of a toddler sitting on his father's knee. The father has his arms wrapped around him as he talks to him. In the father's back are four large arrows. The soul of a father is to protect. My respect for Joe soars, being a parent I understand.

Family put love into life. I would do anything to protect mine, even live forty years with the feeling that something is missing.

The refrigerator is clean and neatly stacked with hearty foods. This surprises me and quickly escalates my opinion of him again. I've always assumed his slim build was due to lack of proper nourishment, it would seem I don't know him as well as I think.

His home mirrors his fridge: crisp, clean, neat, and not overly manly. Coasters on the coffee table are another eyebrow-raising moment for me. He takes care of his home as well as his body. It's an odd sensation knowing how little I know him.

I'm drawn to a framed photograph on the mantel. Joe has his arms wrapped around Freddie, his love for his son plain to see.

I turn to find Joe watching me. 'You're all grown up,' I smile.

'Come with me.' He offers his hand and we enter the bedroom.

I should be having second thoughts. I should leave.

I kick off my shoes.

August heat fills the room, sweat is trickling down my back, but I think my temperature has more to do with lust than heat. Joe turns on the ceiling fan and its cooling breeze brings relief.

Joe's smile is brimming with desire. It's infectious and my temperature rises even more.

In the bedroom, we stand still and just look at each other. His face has gone curiously sober.

'Have you changed your mind?' I ask.

'I'm just marveling at the fact that you're here.'

Something intangible creeps over my flesh.

'I've dreamed of this moment for a long time.'

'This is just a one-off, Joe.'

'As you say.'

'I mean it.'

'I know you do.' With force he pulls me to him. I slam into his body with a gasp. 'I plan to make you change your mind.' Before I can answer, his lips claim mine. They're firm and demanding. My insides go crazy.

Why am I here?

What mysterious force has propelled me into this alternative reality? Why don't I leave before it's too late? Why?

Thoughts fade and are no longer able to form.

Feeling is everything.

Sensations control my responses to his inquisitive hands. Burning between my legs tells me this is where I want to be.

I give as good as I get. My hands hungrily touch his flesh; my lips frantically cover him with kisses.

Clothes drop to the floor; we slip between his cotton-cool sheets. A high-pitched tone rings in my temples blocking out everything except desire.

There is no foreplay. Our hunger is too great, demanding the most intimate of all connections – the coming together of flesh *and* souls. We melt into each other, he gives me all of himself, and I give him all of me. We are truly one – for one and a half minutes!

'Sorry,' he gushes.

I laugh. The joy of the supposedly 'wicked' action bubbles and overflows.

He leans up on his elbow and grins down at me. 'If I didn't have thick skin, I might be a bit cheesed off that you're laughing at me right now!'

'How long do you need?' I ask, waggling my eyebrows at him.

Laughter bursts from him; it's the intoxicating sound of delight. 'Twenty minutes,' he chortles.

Oh, the blessedness of youth!

We talk about everything and nothing. He pumps me with questions, interrogating my soul out of its shell, until I'm revealing things that I'd squashed and buried for years. The open honesty in my replies surprises me and encourages Joe to delve deeper.

'Describe me,' he demands with hushed anticipation.

From his demeanor, I know this is an important question to him, maybe the most important one he's ever asked. 'What do you mean?' I ask, playing for time to think.

'Tell me what you know about me.'

I flick through memories of his youth spent with us. 'You like football, and you support Manchester United.'

Disappointment flickers in his irises. 'No, that's not what I want to hear. *Who* am I?'

Before the party and hand-holding night, I had a clear image of who he was: a loving father, a kindhearted soul, and a good friend to my son. But so much has changed since the party. I no longer see the shell, I see the pearl inside.

'You're passionate and loyal. You're a giver and a taker. On the outside you look calm and composed, but inside you're a volcano of burning emotions. You're more secretive than I knew, and much more romantic than I could have ever guessed.'

His breath is sucked in on a hiss, he reaches for me.

'I've not finished.'

His pupils are fully dilated, red veins flush the whites of his eyes, his desire is coming off him in waves.

'You're mysterious. A therapist and a loving father, you like stability, routines, and home life. Yet, you're here, crushing all realms of social respectability, which leads me to believe that something taboo awakens your passion. Do I know you?'

'You missed out that I don't play around. I don't believe in affairs or flings. I need commitment.'

I bristle and try to detangle myself from his arms. He pins me down.

'If that's true, then why am I here? You can receive nothing from me but an affair. I will never commit to you.'

'Ask me.'

'Ask you what?' I bark, still struggling for release.

'To describe you.'

I go still in his arms. Do I want to know? I don't think so. I purse my lips.

He laughs. 'You're a puzzle to solve. Outwardly mumsy, hiding behind brown skirts and bulky jumpers, thinking no one will notice your sexuality – which burns within you with a bright light. You're a giver, loving, kind and thoughtful. But you're so god-damn sad it breaks my heart.'

'I'm not at all!'

'But you are. You hide behind smiles, but I *see* you, Rose, surrounded by people who love you and yet incredibly lonely. You wear a hair shirt with pride.'

'I do not!'

'Self-sacrificing in all that you do. For years you have looked like a dying bouquet that's wilting from lack of water. I never knew I could be that water for you, never guessed that you might desire me the way I have done you for years. But I knew something was missing in your life. You need me Rose, let me love you back to life.'

We may have waited longer than twenty minutes, but his hardness presses against me now. All the while he's been talking his hands have roamed my flesh. Despite the anger that brims in my mind, my body has been responding to him.

Shivers ripple over me, my hips rise of their own accord – oh treacherous body!

He slides across me, I wish I was slim. When he guides himself inside me, I'm ready.

The frantic edge to our earlier coupling has gone. Joe is in control, he rearranges us, bringing us closer together and then pulls back. He repeats again and again.

When it is over, I'm in a place where I've never been before – I'm satisfied. Every inch of me has melted with pleasure.

I think I'm in love! Well, in love with *this* anyway. This feeling of being alive and eternally young, of being desired and fully appreciated as a woman, oh yes, with *this* I'm truly in love.

We're cuddling, flesh against flesh, and waves of loss wash over me. This is another thing I miss, this closeness and connection.

How I'm happy for Joe to see my chubby body is a mystery to me. Maybe it's because he doesn't seem to mind, in fact he seems to rather like it – he certainly is touching it enough.

I like his posture; it is somehow pleasing to me. The youth of him makes my stomach contract; yes I like it a lot. He's so slim I'm tempted to fatten him up a little. His flesh is hard and muscular, but his touch is soft and gentle.

My mind is protesting my current situation, but I pay it as much attention as I would a worm beneath the ground. I'm lost now. Consumed by Joe. His hand is exploring my body again like a child dives into presents on Christmas morning. His hunger pulsates off him in waves of heat making me giddy.

I wonder if he's noticed that my legs are a little too short or that my ankles are slightly swollen. Does he see my age? Does he notice my maturity when he touches my flesh? Am I abhorrent to him really? Is this just lust? Will he disappear from my life as soon as I leave? So many questions, no answers, just feelings and sensations and a dawning hope that this will never end.

The wrinkles on my hands remind me of all the times I've hugged and loved. They show I have worked and lived, and are the evidence of my life and age. I love them, but right now I'm wondering what Joe thinks of them.

Dancing in the Garden of Love

MY PLAYLIST HAS CHANGED over the last few months... since the party. I'm peeling potatoes when *I am a Women in Love* by *Barbara Streisand* comes on. I hold the sink and close my eyes. Visions come to mind. Flashes. Moments. All of them recalling Joe. I let go of the sink and raise my arms.

I feel like dancing.

I sway. I take a step. I sway. I twirl.

I sing at the top of my lungs... 'And I'd do anything, to get you into my world.' *(Barbara Streisand 1980)*

I am ageless.

Joe desires me, a man desires me!

'No truth is ever a lie, I stumble and fall. But I give you it all...'

Inside me, vitality bubbles with the freshness of a babbling brook. I twirl again. My arms wave and weave through the air. I am young. I am attractive. There are no laughter lines around my eyes. No double-chin. No swollen ankles. No hurting knees. No aching back.

The song changes; *Ronan Keating's If Tomorrow Never Comes* has started. I go in the cupboard and bring out the mop. I turn it upside down.

'Why thank you, I'd love to.' I play coy with the mop bristles, feigning shyness. Then I swing wide and begin my million-bubbles-of-joy dance with my imaginary partner. 'Joe,' I laugh, 'you *really* need a haircut.' I shake the mop making the bristles bob up and down.

Savage Garden's Truly, Madly, Deeply comes on. I put the mop down and just dance. Aches and pains forgotten, I move like I used to do… when I was young, and without a care for how I looked or what people thought.

When I was young…

I switch off the music and sit down. I'm no longer young, I'm past middle-aged and on the slow decline to the end. God how depressing! Is that why Joe has gotten under my skin?

I need to see him again. I can't wait until Saturday morning as agreed. I scribble a note and grab my keys. I'll push the note under his door, see what he says.

When I get home I feel daring, reckless. Part of me doesn't care, another part is petrified.

I don't hear from Joe that day. I'm disappointed; although we've agreed no texts I'm wondering if I should send him one. I don't. Too much risk.

The next morning the house phone rings.

'Hi.'

My heart thumps. 'Hi.'

'Is *he* home?'

'Yes.'

'OK, just pretend I'm calling to ask you how you make your Fisherman's Pie.'

'Oh, it's easy. Yes, I always use two tins of tuna.'

'I want to see you too.'

'Yes, four soft-boiled eggs.'

'I want to undress you and do naughty things with you.'

My stomach's going crazy. 'You mash the eggs in the tuna.'

'I can't wait for Saturday either. Can you come around after work on Wednesday?'

'I don't know. Finely chop parsley and add that, and then make a roux sauce.'

'Wednesday evening is the only time I'm free. If you can't come we'll meet on Saturday like planned.'

'Pour the sauce into the tuna, add a good measure of salt and pepper.'

'I'm going to do wicked things with you, I'm going to make you scream.'

My knees have gone weak. 'You tip the mixture onto puff pastry and fold the pastry over to make a box.'

'I want you, Rose.'

'I forgot to say keep half the parsley for the sauce!' My voice is slightly high-pitched.

'Do whatever you can to come on Wednesday. If you can't make it, I'll see you Saturday, you sexy thing.'

'OK. Just bake for forty-five minutes in a moderate oven.'

'See you soon.'

'Yes, that's it; serve with boiled potatoes, peas and a parsley sauce. Bye then.'

I'm trembling when I put the phone down.

'Was that Joe?'

I nearly jump out of my skin! How long has he been standing there? Could he hear Joe? I'm trying to stay calm, but heat is flushing my cheeks.

'Yes, just wanted the fish pie recipe.'

'I didn't know he did much cooking.'

'Apparently, Freddie's had it here a few times and asked him to make it.' Liar, liar, pants on fire. When did I become this woman?

'Umm.' Harvey's face doesn't look convinced but he goes back to the study, his den.

I decide to do a bit of weeding in the garden to keep busy. The whole time I'm pulling them up, or dead-heading the roses I'm trying to come up with a reason why I would suddenly want to go out, on my own, on a Wednesday night. In the end, I decide to take a risk.

Two days later and Wednesday is here. I wait all day until we're eating dinner and then I ask.

'I think I'm going to go to the pictures after dinner. There's a new film of *West Side Story* on. Do you want to come with me?' I know full well that he hates musicals; still it's a gamble he doesn't say yes or question why I'm going in the evening when I usually go to matinees.

I think he answers before he thinks about it. 'No, not for me that stuff.' Then he pulls a funny face like maybe he should have said yes.

I rush ahead before he changes his mind. 'I'm quite looking forward to it. It starts at seven, so I'll be home around nine-thirty.' I start clearing the dinner table.

'Do you want me to come with you?'

That's a veiled question if ever there was one. I have to answer like I always do. 'You know I would love you to come with me, but I know you don't like musicals. Why don't we go and see the new *James Bond* film, *No Time to Die* next week?'

'Yeah, I quite fancy that one.'

I smile out of the kitchen window as I wash the dishes. My husband is rather predictable. I have had a pay-monthly cinema pass now for three years, ever since I retired. I go by myself all the time. I love the cinema, just as much as books. At first I used to ask him to come with me all the time, in the end I stopped asking and just went on my own. After the first few times I became totally relaxed going solo, I even enjoy not having to talk to anyone when I go for my secret pleasure. Over time the cinema staff have come to know me and greet me by name now, it's nice. What Harvey doesn't know is that I went to see *West Side Story* last week, so if he asks me about it I'll be ready with the answers, not that he ever asks me if I enjoyed a film, it's like he doesn't even notice when I go out of the house anymore.

Except today I feel his eyes on me. Is my guilt giving off weird vibes?

I kiss him on the head, play nonchalant and head off. My heart is pounding. I've become *that* other woman, something I'd never thought I'd be. In fact, I have been known to be rather verbal in my opinion of people who cheat, and yet here I am. Driving with quite some speed towards my lover, too excited to stop and analyze what I'm doing.

'Hi,' says Joe as he opens the door for me.

'Hi.'

I had been brave right up until knocking on his door. Now I just feel nervous. He hands me a glass of white wine. 'Thanks.'

'I was going to pounce on you Mrs. Delaney, but you look a bit fragile. Come on in and sit down.'

His playful tone and easy manner make me feel better. 'I have to leave before nine-fifteen.'

'Where are you supposed to be?'

'Watching a film.'

'Which one?'

'*West Side Story*.'

'I never like remakes much, though I hear it's supposed to be quite good.'

'It is, I saw it last week.'

'What did you enjoy?'

Joe puts his arm around me and we settle in next to each other. I'm happy as I share my opinions of the film, it's good that someone is interested in my thoughts.

When I finish talking, Joe takes the glass from my hand and puts it on the table. Then he moves in, slowly and surely, and pulls my face to his. His lips are soft. Bubbles of joy are rising to my chest. I love the way he kisses me. Powerful, determined, claiming my lips as his own. I've never been kissed like this before.

Before long he is leading me into the bedroom.

We undress, facing each other. He wants to play as we stand, naked as the day we were born. I want to hide my body and insist on getting between the sheets.

He kisses my cheek, my neck, my cleavage.

I push my hips against him. I need him inside me.

He grins a wolfish seductive claim stating he has me. 'Maybe I'm too sexy for my boots!'

'You don't lack confidence, that's for sure.'

'Not with you.'

That gives me pause. 'You lack confidence elsewhere?'

'Don't we all?'

'Yes, I suppose we do.'

Joe rubs a thumb over my lips. 'You surprise me.'

'Why's that?'

'In all the years I've daydreamed of you, I never in my wildest imagination thought you would be so... adventurous.'

'Some things should remain a mystery you know.'

After that Joe takes control and leads us in the timeless dance of lovers. A short time later we flop happily exhausted and let our fire burn low.

A few minutes of silent cuddling pass, and then I ask, 'How did things change between us? I mean, I've known you nearly all your life. Why now? What made you make a move?'

'Your hunger.'

'What?'

'That night, when I wrapped my arms around your waist, I was being cheeky. Touching you when everyone would assume it was pure affection. But... you turned and looked up at me.' Joe's breath catches and causes a hiss to escape his lips as he recalls the image. 'Your eyes were eating me. You lit a torch to my desire and I wanted nothing more right then but to lay you down and take you right then and there, and I couldn't care less for the consequences.'

'Joe!' I slap his chest. His rashness unnerves me.

'Sorry, Rose.'

I can't look at him. It's time to go.

'Rose, I'm sorry... but you asked.'

'I shouldn't have. And I shouldn't be here.'

If only the world could remain hidden, but it has crept back in and is demanding to be taken seriously. One after another daily thoughts pop into my melted aura and drag me back towards my responsibilities.

'I need to go.'

Joe tightens his grip on me. 'Two hours isn't enough.'

I can't argue with him. Like a petulant child I want more. 'In the middle of September, he's going to Dubai for a two-week golf tournament.'

Joe leans over me, excitement in his eyes. His skin is sleek with salty sweat. 'And?'

'I was wondering if we could go on holiday.'

'You and me?'

There's a lump in my throat. This is a big step, maybe a step too far. I nod.

Joe leaps out of bed and starts pulling on his boxers. 'Where do you want to go?'

'Somewhere with a swimming pool.'

'Budget?'

'As low as possible.'

'That shouldn't be a problem. Last minute deals can be great value. Have you ever been to Greece?'

'I went to Rhodes as a child.'

'I'll look for something for us. Leave it with me.'

'I've got to book my own holiday, Joe. He sees all payments; I don't have a private bank account.'

'No problem. We'll find something and sort it out as we go.'

Joe watches me as I dress; with the weather being so hot I only have a shapeless cotton dress on. I feel self-conscious like I should be making more of an effort for my lover. But I can hardly start buying provocative clothes now; Harvey would know in an instant that something was going on. The thought delivers sadness to my chest. I feel trapped, caged. After forty years of marriage, I want to be free. I think it's time for some new clothes.

We walk to the front door together, just as we reach it Joe pulls me into him. Surprise makes me laugh, and then his hungry kisses make my lips tender as he claims them as his own.

'Rose, Rose,' he murmurs while smothering my face and hair with kisses.

'Stop, I've got to get home.'

'I don't want to stop.'

'Joe!'

'OK. OK.' He drops his hands to his sides and takes a step back. 'You'd best go before I drag you back to bed!'

I flee before his longing consumes my senses. As I rush down the steps to the car park, the 'other woman' with all her name tags returns, and firmly shoves the 'new' Rose out of the way. As I drive I pull on all my skill and compose myself, as if nothing untoward at all has happened.

Who is this deceitful woman who hides under my skin?

Truly, Madly, Deeply

THERE IS SOMETHING INFINITELY sad and poignant about this affair, and surprisingly it isn't the fact that I'm cheating on my husband, it's because I can't trust my own feelings.

Do I *really* love Joe?

Or is it that I love feeling young again?

Or is it because he makes me feel treasured and attractive?

Maybe, if I could clearly define why I love Joe, I could make different decisions. I want to *know* that I'm not going crazy. I wish I could live beyond what I deem is right and respectable. I wish I could still love and care for my family *and* keep seeing Joe.

Part of me wants to run away. Live a dream, and experience a different more selfish kind of life. But neither of us can leave our children, it's not in our nature. The alternative, to stay and tell everyone, would be too painful. Leaving my husband would break him. I can't be that callous.

The only way forward is for this affair to end.

I must be strong.

When Joe opens his door, I'm struck with the thought that he might have gypsy blood in his veins. His soft curly hair frames his face, which is well-tanned. He has a gold earring in his left ear. His jeans are faded, his loafers comfy and his fisherman's style blue jumper speaks volumes to how comfortable he is in his own skin.

We hug. He's clean and fresh, smelling of musk and cinnamon. He is everything I like in a man; unassuming, quiet and exceedingly confident, with just a touch of mischief and merry eyes.

I shouldn't be here, but I'm delighted I am. He makes us coffee, never taking his eyes off me. I'm filled with the fancy that he has lived many lives already and that in this lifetime he's searching for his eternal partner. He scares me. I cannot be that person, yet I find myself drawn to him, losing myself.

I hover in the doorway.

'You don't want to come in?'

'Can we go for a walk?'

At first his face drops displaying disappointment. He quickly recovers and grins. 'Sure, do you fancy some fun in the woods?' He winks.

'Just a walk.'

His grin softens to a gentle, understanding smile. 'Sure, where do you want to go?'

'The reservoir.'

'Give me a moment to put my boots on. Do you want to go together or in separate cars?'

'I think it would be best to go separately. If anyone sees us we can say we met there by chance.'

'OK. You go on ahead then, I'll be right behind you.'

It's a twenty-five-minute drive there and the whole time I wonder what I'm doing. Just a walk I tell myself repeatedly.

From days long gone, I automatically drive to a quiet lane where you can cut across a footpath and join the reservoir at its north end; a place quite overgrown with few visitors. When I pull in I berate myself for not confirming with Joe which part I would park at. I'm wondering if he'll head straight to the car park. But five minutes later his Ford is pulling in behind me. I sigh in relief.

We both get out of the car at the same time. Heading across the public footpath Joe takes my hand. 'No one around,' he winks.

'I wasn't sure you'd remember where I come,' I say after we climb the stile and make our way down to the water.

'I remember everything about you, Rose. A short distance from here is a clearing where you always brought us for picnics. You said it was like Heaven on Earth.'

'You've got a good memory.'

'Hmm.'

We walk for a while in silence, and I'm glad the pathways are empty. We reach the stone wall skirting the edge of the water and lean against it, looking out and absorbing the beauty of nature.

'What's on your mind, Rose?'

'I love being with you.'

He turns to me and pushes a stray wisp of hair off my face. 'I feel a but coming.'

His touch thrills me. I change my mind, I can't say goodbye just yet. Instead, I reach up and pull his face to mine. Instantly, his arms are around me. This is home, this is where I want to be.

As with all new lovers, our ardor is quick to surface.

Joe grabs my hand and pulls me into the thicket.

I can't believe what we're about to do. Joe finds a spot of soft moss and lies me down. We waste no time and lose ourselves in passion.

NOBODY IS PERFECT UNTIL you fall in love with them, that's what they say, but I would have added more to that sentence. I would have said that you know when you're in love when you can see the person isn't perfect, but you love them regardless. Isn't that what it's all about?

That's what I maintained throughout my marriage. Harvey isn't perfect and neither am I. We're just comfortable with each other. We're kind and considerate and like the routine of having someone you care about to talk to each day. Isn't friendship the best basis for a marriage? Isn't that what it's all about?

Only now I'm *in* love my thinking has changed, because Joe appears perfect to me. I love everything about him. I've searched for faults and I can't find any.

His cleft chin is my only cause of concern. I've noticed Joe tenses, and those reflexes cause him to tighten his jaw. I don't think he's aware that he does it. If I close my eyes and search my memories, I can see him doing it as a child. Something would happen or something would be said, he'd freeze for a fraction of a second and then relax, almost like he thought that everything that happened to him or around him might offer him harm and he tensed to fight it off. Realizing everything was alright he would relax... and smile. To this day he still does it, but it is so minimal that you would have to be staring at him intently and continually to be able to pick it up. I guess I've been doing a lot of that lately. It's not that he's afraid; I think it's a reflex, a habit from his childhood he hasn't been able to drop. It's quite at odds to his super laid-back, relaxed persona, but it's there – a shadow of pain that haunts him.

I've decided I love everything about him, but some things more than others. I love the way he loves his son, so passionately and completely, he literally oozes happiness whenever he talks about Freddie. I love the way he always wants to touch me. There are a hundred things I could say about that. But I think the thing I love the most is the way he locks eyes with me and never wants to turn away. We bare our souls to each other, it's intoxicating stuff.

THERE IS SOMETHING ABOUT kissing in the rain that is pure. The sky tilts its water and soaks us. Teasingly, the sun peeks through clouds. It could have rained at any time; it seems deliberate that the clouds emptied right now, as we sneak a Sunday afternoon walk into our lives yet again breaking our Saturday-mornings only rule.

The earth throws up damp wafts of mud and moss, and leaves glisten as water trickles over them.

Neither of us runs for cover. We move closer together as rain bounces on the ground around our feet. Within moments we are drenched.

Joe slips his hand under the soaking blouse that clings to my body. He fans his fingers across my back. I run my hand under his t-shirt and stroke the hairs on his chest. Our foreheads touch. I stare at his lips.

Joe moves us, artfully, like a master dancer, one step then two. I don't look where we're going as my eyes remain on his lips.

My back is against a tree. Thick branches protect us from the summer downpour. Joe's hand is moving, going up my leg under my skirt.

Standing, at one with nature, uncaring for being exposed, Joe makes love to me, pushing me against the bark with his need to connect.

A rainbow appears as the sun bursts through a break in the clouds, and hope fills us with its eternal desire of happiness. Love glistens on the edge of the rainbow, sprinkling its magic over us. Powerful and life-changing it blossoms in our souls as it has in others throughout time.

I don't know the how or why, nor can I explain its calling. All I know is that love breaks down boundaries and demands our eternal submission to its calling.

Love is changing me.

There should be a separate word for this type of love, because we love in so many different ways that simply saying love seems to do *this* no justice at all.

How lucky am I to be alive right now, to experience this wondrous thing! How green are the leaves on the towering oaks, how crisply I see the veins that flow through them. I am lost in an ocean of endless song. I soar like an eagle and dance upon the stars. They are mere stepping stones on my path to love. I am outside of my body. I fall. I drown. I am in the heart of my soul. I soar once more and float above the clouds. I am with the angels, I hear them sing.

It is too much to contain. I must confess.

I am truly, madly, deeply in love with Joe.

Scorpion

I AM LOST. SET ADRIFT from shore, reliant upon the good nature of the current to bring me home safely. I am unconventional. I see the awful bad taste of being involved in a physical relationship with a boy half my age. Although, Joe's not a boy, but separating years of watching him grow up with this unfathomable attraction is hard.

It seems to me, with the shift of my weight from left to right, that one moment he is impossibly young and the next more mature than my old college professor.

We've been for a long walk. Joe's presence fills me with happiness. Sharing our appreciation seems to heighten our wonder of the place. The reservoir has become 'our place' and we never tire of its beauty. Yet on the walk back my joy is battered by my guilt.

I'm profoundly infatuated with this boy/man, this sexual beast who proclaims to only have eyes for me. Who lays me down upon the grass and ravishes me. Is he wickedly clever telling me all the things my dried-up soul longs to hear? Or is he inexplicably naïve and baring his soul to me? Whoever he is, he's hooked me and drawn me to a place so delectably wicked that a part of me is drowning.

'You look glum.'

How attuned to me he is.

'This is wrong, Joe.' I wave a finger between us. 'We need to stop before someone gets hurt.'

'It's your marriage that's wrong, Rose, not us.'

'Don't you feel guilty?'

Joe stops and I stop with him. He takes both my hands in his. He pauses for a moment, weighing up how I will respond. 'I am not the married one, Rose. You're the one that has broken your marriage vows.'

I pull air in through my nose and try to let go of his hands. He grips them tighter. 'You can't run away from the truth. You entered into a contract with your husband, stating that boundaries shouldn't be broken, and because of that you are filled with guilt. I wish I could take it away from you but I can't. As to me and my guilt, you're going to be disappointed with my answer. Do I wish that our being together wouldn't hurt anyone else, yes, do I feel guilty for loving you, no. All I know is that you have stepped out of your marriage and broken that bond. That shows me that there is something missing in your marriage Rose, because I *know* you. And I know you aren't doing this lightly. Being with me is life-changing for you, I know that. But I'm sorry, I don't feel guilty.'

I don't know what to say. My burden is heavy. We head back to the car in silence. 'Let's sit in my car for a while.'

We get in but Joe turns his head away from me and looks out his window for a moment, before turning back to me. 'I might not be consumed with guilt, but I'm painfully aware of my failings. It rather puts me off seeking new relationships, because frankly I'm afraid of rejection. So when I pursued you, Rose, it wasn't on a whim or a fancy. It wasn't a game. I'm serious about you. I want you in my life, and I think you want me too. You're just too scared to let go of the past and face the future on a new path.'

'Fear is both a terrible thing, and a necessary evil. Where would we be without its reins? Fear is good, I'm grateful for it.'

'Rose!' Those raised eyebrows frame his all-consuming stare, that burrowing into my soul and calling my bluff.

'Which one of us is allowing fear to steal our joy? You always told us we should never let fear steal our joy.'

'Can't you go back to being a skinny, knock-kneed boy who always did what I said?'

'You'd be arrested if I did!' His eyes are laughing at me.

'I should be arrested now!'

'Don't be silly, and besides I'd never let anyone harm you, I'd whisk you away and keep you safe.'

Isn't that what every woman wants? Here it is being offered to me and I can't accept it. There is more to life than me. 'We're not in a fairytale.'

'No, we're in the greatest love story ever told.'

'I wish I was free.'

'You're as free as you want to be.'

'But I'm not. I'm embroiled in a life I made for myself. The happiness of my family comes first.'

'They'd get over it, Rose.' I can hear the exasperation in his voice.

'I don't know how to make a decision when I can't see what will happen tomorrow. All I have is what I feel in my gut, and that's telling me that our kids and Harvey will be heartbroken. I can't do it to them.'

'Then stop using me!'

He's so angry! Where did that come from? 'Joe?'

'If leaving him is so impossible for you, stop using me to fulfill your childish daydreams!'

'Joe!' I'm gob-smacked, where did this Joe come from?

'Joe, I'm not doing that.'

He's out of the car already, so I get out and run after him as he goes towards his Ford.

'Joe, please.'

He spins around and his face has a mask on it. It's one that makes me take a step back. 'I don't do games, nor do I do affairs. So if you're not going to even consider leaving him then stay the hell away from me.'

'Well... that's not fair! You're the one who has done all the chasing!'

He opens his car, but before he gets in he turns back to look at me. 'Is that right? Go home and take a good hard look at yourself Rose. Why would I chase you?'

'Ouch!' Oh damn-damn-damn, heck, ouch. I feel sick.

I expect him to say sorry, to take me in his arms and tell me he doesn't mean it. He gets in the car, reverses so hard his tyres screech, and speeds off, leaving me stunned and alone. Drowning, drowning, drowning.

His birthday is the fifth of November, and he's a Scorpio through and through.

***

THIS IS THE THIRD TIME he's been to the house since our bust-up. Each time he's found the door locked. I've peeped behind my bedroom curtains (as I'm doing now) and watched him pacing the driveway. The last two times he gave up after about fifteen minutes and drove off. Today he is hammering my door down. It's a good job ours is a detached house set back a good distance from the road so no one can see or hear him.

Damn golf too, because if my hubby had been here instead of being with his chums, Joe wouldn't be here.

'Let me in, Rose!' He steps back from the door a little and looks straight at me. I jump back and let the curtain drop. He hammers on the door again. 'I'm not going away until you speak with me. So if you want everyone to find out about us this is a good way.'

I rush down the stairs. My hands shake as I unlock the door. When I yank it open I'm glaring at him. 'Go away!'

He pushes past me. 'You should stop saying that. Now get in here.'

I'm fuming; in fact I'm so mad I'm shaking. 'Say what you have to say and get out.'

He turns around. We're in the living room. The blinds are down to keep out the heat but the room is still warm, unbearably so. 'I'm sorry.'

Air whistles out of me like a steam train. I'd been ready to argue, to scream at him and tell him never to darken my door again, but he's just knocked the stuffing out of me. He's sincere, it's plain to see.

A lump is forming in my throat. I've spent the last week verbally bashing myself for being such a stupid woman. Of course a man wouldn't want to chase me. I'm an idiot for thinking one would, especially one so young. Hot tears spring forth.

Joe is with me in an instant. His arms wrap around me and I unashamedly lean in and lay my head on his shoulder.

'I'm sorry Rose, truly I am. I was lashing out, trying to hurt you for not picking me. I didn't mean what I said. It was cruel. Please forgive me, Rose, please.'

How weak am I that I'm just so grateful he's here I can forgive him anything? He strokes my hair and calm descends. Who is the adult here?

Knowing that I've stopped crying, Joe lifts my face by placing a finger under my chin. He rubs his nose against mine. 'Rose, Rose, my precious Rose, do you forgive me?'

I do. And I don't.

'Truth is often spoken in anger.'

'I chased you, of course I did. You never would have broken out of your shell if I hadn't been persistent.'

'That may be so, but nothing has changed. I'm not leaving him to be with you.' There! The truth spoken out loud and clear. I can't honestly say I know why this is the decision I must make, love for my family, or fear for myself, I don't know. But what I do know, without a doubt, is that unless my Harvey asks me to leave, this is where I belong.

'OK.'

'OK?'

'Whatever you say, but I need to know... will you keep on seeing me?'

'But you don't want an affair.'

'I don't, but I want to lose you even less, so if snatched moments with you are all I can have then I want them.'

I should tell him no, I should hesitate at least. 'Yes.'

His brown eyes pierce me. 'Yes... you'll carry on seeing me.'

'Yes.'

We snatch a forbidden kiss right then, right here in the middle of my house, the house where I live with my husband, the house where my children grew up. Right in the middle of it I stand defiant and resolute. I want this. I might not be able to leave my husband, but at the moment I also don't want to lose Joe.

I REFUSE TO SEE JOE ALL WEEK. But Saturday mornings have become our special time, before he goes to pick up Freddy, before I start the evening meal. We've allotted ourselves three hours of just him and me. Each minute is precious, stolen and treasured. I don't think it's enough for either of us, but it's all I'll allow to happen from now on. No more taking risks of being seen by going on walks, no matter how much we both enjoy them.

His flat has become comfortable to me. When I'm daydreaming I think about living here. I imagine we'd be happy, but remind myself that dreams rarely come true. We spend all our time listening to music. Sometimes we sing along, especially when we're making brunch together, other times we dance. We listen as we make love. I listen when I grab a shower. Joe serenades me all the time. Our short time together is filled with musical happiness.

Despite his angular features and thin frame, everything about Joe is soft. With a disarming smile and a perpetual glisten in his eyes, he is dynamically attractive, in an unassuming way. His self-effacing jokes clearly state his impression of himself, but he can't see what I see. Funny how we only see the worst in ourselves. Yet when he sings he's full of confidence. I love it when he sings as his lips are roaming my body, because I know he is happy.

We're lying on our backs, looking at the ceiling.

Joe's finger strokes my thigh absentmindedly. 'How long can we last, Rose?'

Aspects of Love

'Our connection will pass away and fade into yesteryear, eventually. Loyalty will endure; it will continue and finish the race. I made a commitment, versed an oath in church, and picked my path. Despite being here with you, being fickle isn't me. I was happy until the moment we connected.' My hands are moving to my words, dramatizing my speech.

'Do you think you can go backwards, pretend we didn't happen? Can you really be happy again?'

'I have to try.'

'I'm going to struggle with this, Rose. I've got to be honest. I think you're going to make the biggest mistake of your life if you don't take a chance on us.'

And so our debate moves back and forth, a tango of emotions, a dance of love above which floats the essence of tragedy with flavors of *Wuthering Heights* and *Romeo and Juliet*. Not that anyone would be interested in our story which is as mundane as love itself. We are just another couple of pebbles on a world covered with pebbles. We don't stand out; we don't glisten brighter than any other. We are so damn normal and clichéd it breaks my heart.

Life-long companionship matters. What I have in my marriage might not suit others, and they may wonder why I stay. Prison sentences are less than my forty years of commitment. Most of the time, I'm grateful for my life but now and again it seems like house arrest. Is this what feeling old does to you? Turn everything that once was sweet to bitter?

'The thought of causing my family pain crushes me.'

'But hurting me doesn't?'

'It does, Joe, of course it does.' I snuggle into his chest. These Saturday mornings are supposed to be about fun and being naughty. Why do I keep destroying it with my insistence on saying we should not be together?

'Your kids are grown up, they'll understand. They'll want you to be happy.'

'That may be, but life would never be the same again. The thought of them spending one Christmas with me and the next with their dad makes me feel awful. The family would be broken. I don't want that for my family.'

'You're killing me.'

'I'm being honest.'

His thumb rubs my shoulder. 'I love my mum, but when I was growing up I wanted to be a part of your family.'

I roll my head and kiss his chest. I understand.

'It seemed to me that you were exactly what a family should be. Your home was always so warm, comfortable and inviting. My mum worked her socks off to keep a roof over our heads, and boy do I love and admire her. But our home never smelled of cookies, nor did our rooms roar with laughter. Our flat was always quiet, subdued compared to yours.'

'Your mum held down two jobs though, didn't she? There wouldn't have been much time for baking. And having no siblings was the reason why your rooms were quiet.'

'Jake kind of adopted me at school you know.'

'He did?'

'Yeah. I was sad after my dad died, and I didn't want to talk to anyone. I used to imagine I was traveling through a world where I didn't exist. It lessened the pain somehow to think I wasn't real. I used to sit on my own all the time but Jake just kept turning up next to me. Eventually, I got used to him and one day accepted his continual offers to come back to yours for tea after school.'

'He's got a big heart that son of mine.'

'He does.'

We're silent for a while; no doubt he's thinking the same as me. Loyalty is not something that should be easily tossed aside. For if we can do that, what kind of people are we?

'I think I'll always love you, Rose.'

'I've loved you since you were a young boy, that won't change.'

'It already has.'

In a silent agreement we get out of bed and get dressed. It's time for me to go home.

LATER, WHILE I'M TRYING to go to sleep, I go over and over our conversations, trying to ascertain the real reason I won't commit to Joe.

I've come to the conclusion that fears hold me back.

Why am I so afraid?

Fear seems to be influencing all the different paths I could take.

Fear – that what Joe and I are experiencing isn't true love but a mixture of wants and desires.

Fear – that Joe will wake up one morning, realize I am old and leave me. I'll end up spending the rest of my life alone. That's not something I would cope well with.

Fear – that my children will take offence and decide to support their dad, which will mean they cut me out of their lives. Maybe a bit irrational, but again, not something I would be able to live with.

Fear – that I'm more in love with feeling young and being desired than I'm in love with Joe.

Fear – what if Harvey can't live without me?

I bolt upright in bed. The other thoughts had been making me melancholy but this thought just rocked something inside me that's now exploding. I sob. The thought that I could make him so sad that he wouldn't want to live anymore is breaking me down into millions of tiny particles. I wrap my arms around my middle and rock back and forth as I sob. Oh no, oh no, I couldn't do that. I couldn't cause that. My sweet man doesn't deserve that.

Resolution descends, like another person entering my body, bringing clarity. Joe and I are temporary. This is an affair that has an expiration date; we must not go beyond it.

THE SMELL OF BACON DRAWS Harvey into the kitchen; I plan to 'feed' him my love and appreciation.

'Good morning,' I chirp. Too cheerful, tone it down!

'Morning.' He kisses me on the forehead and sits at the table.

'Smells good,' he says, picking up the newspaper.

'You can't beat the smell of bacon, coffee and fresh baked bread, they've got to be my favorite top three smells.'

'You like vanilla too, don't you?'

It shouldn't surprise me that he knows something about me, we have been married for forty years after all, and yet it does.

I serve him a sandwich and then fetch the pot of tea. His first drink of the day is always tea, mine is coffee.

'What do you have planned for today?'

He lowers the paper slightly and peers at me over the top. 'Nothing special. You?'

'I was wondering if we could maybe look at holidays?'

'You've booked one haven't you?'

Why does he have to be so sharp? 'Yes I have, but I was hoping we could book one for the two of us. It's been a few years now since we've gone away... together.'

'Are you having a dig at me, Rose?'

'No, of course not. Why would I do that?'

He puts the paper down on the table and looks at me, his face is unreadable. My heart is racing as I wait for his response. Why is he so cross?

'You think because I go to Scotland and Dubai every year that I don't want to go away with you.'

'It's crossed my mind!'

'And that's why you've decided to go off to Santorini on your own, not even taking one of your friends with you.'

My body is trembling. I hate confrontation. I put my hands on my lap so he can't see that they're shaking. 'Actually, in my book my main character is having an affair.

I'm sending them to Santorini for a holiday together, so I thought it would be good for me to go and research the place, try and capture the essence of it.'

A flicker of something I don't understand goes across his face. When he speaks his voice is lower, softer. 'Don't you think you'll be uncomfortable going everywhere on your own?'

'I've done a lot of research.' I really had. 'Quite a lot of single people travel Europe on their own, the majority are backpackers, but some stay in hotels. It's why I've picked the cheapest hotel; it has a reputation for single people being comfortable there. When I'm not out and about taking pictures, I want to sit by the pool and write. The reviews say that no one bothers you in Perissa Bay. I'm sure I'll be just fine.'

'You don't want to ask Gemma if she'd like to go with you? We'd pay for her of course.'

'I want to go on my own.'

'I bet you do.'

'What does that mean? You can't begrudge me one small holiday? Tell me, exactly how much is it costing for you to stay at your five-star hotel in Dubai?'

He stands up, folds his newspaper under his arm then picks up his plate and cup. 'I don't know what's got into you lately Rose, but I don't like it. I'm going to my office for some peace and quiet.'

I watch his back with stings of angry tears in my eyes. So much for loving him as much as possible!

I LOVE MY GIRLFRIENDS. We've been partners in crime since we met when our children were young.

Daphne's on her third marriage, I don't know how she does it, but she has such a zest for life that men are drawn to her like bees to nectar.

Melody's husband left her for his secretary, (there's a lot I can say about that, but I'll refrain). She proclaims she is happy being single and loves her space and making her own decisions. I think she's been badly scarred and just doesn't trust men now.

Darla's husband Mike, died of prostate cancer two years ago, which was terribly sad, he'd had a slow decline over seven years. It left Darla sad beyond measure and exhausted both mentally and physically. She doesn't think there will be anyone else for her, and I think she's right. She loved John with her whole being, I don't think there's space for anyone else.

These three ladies have been my rock for years. My go-to when I need support or fun. I'm surprised that I'm unable to share what's going on with me with them. I don't know why I can't tell them. Shame? I think I'll tell them, and then I just can't open my mouth. I guess I don't want them to think badly of me.

We're sitting in a cozy café sipping cappuccinos. They've just finished telling me what a great time they'd had in the Lakes. I smile and nod. If I had been with them I might have had the courage to walk away from Joe by now. Maybe if I told them they would talk me out of this madness.

'So come on,' says Daphne, 'what's going on with you?'

Now or never.

'Nothing, what do you mean?'

Melody tuts. 'Oh come on Rose, you're just not yourself at all. One minute you're glowing and there's this sparkle in your eye, and the next you look like you've been given ten days to live.'

I flick my eyes to Darla; death is a touchy subject.

She chooses to ignore it. 'Spill the beans,' she says with a weary smile.

'I think I must be having a late menopause or something.'

'Oh, give me a break!' laughs Daphne. 'You went through that years ago.'

'Isn't there such a thing as a late one? A last-minute attempt of your body to scream it wants to stay young?'

'Is everything OK between you and Harvey?' Of course Melody would assume he was cheating on me.

'He doesn't seem to be himself recently, he's got awfully snappy with me, I don't know why.'

'It could be guilt,' says Melody. 'Kevin was always picking fights with me before he left.'

'Yes, but he's nothing like Kevin, I can't believe for a minute he would cheat on Rose,' says Daphne – the woman I'm sure has secretly been in love with my husband for years.

Darla shuffles in her chair like she's uncomfortable. 'Maybe he's not well and doesn't want to tell you. Mike didn't tell me for a long time.' She sighs.

'He doesn't look ill, and I've not noticed him eating less than normal or anything, in fact I'd say he's been eating more.'

'Maybe he hates the fact that you're going on holiday on your own?' offers Daphne. She raises one eyebrow at me. I can see that she's wondering why on earth I'm having a solo holiday at this time in my life when I've never had one before.

'He seemed OK about it when I told him I wanted to go.'

'Yes, but is he *really*?' adds Daphne leaning across the table. 'Some men just can't show their emotions you know. Maybe he secretly hates that you're going away without him?'

'He goes away without me!' I don't mean to be sharp but it comes out that way.

Daphne sits back in her seat. 'OK, spill the beans girl, what's going on with you?'

I start to cry. It's a self-protection mechanism.

They're instantly around me, cuddles galore, with lots of 'there-there' and 'hush, it'll be OK.' They don't even know what's wrong.

When they've sat down and I've blown my nose, Melody lays a hand on my arm. 'Now you have to tell us, we're all worried about you.'

'I'm an emotional mess. I don't know what's wrong, honest I don't. All I know is that I want to be young again. I want to have a second chance at life and start over. Do things differently. I love my kids; I would still get married because I don't want a start-over without them. But when they started leaving home, maybe at that point I should have chosen something else for me.'

They're all looking at me like I'm mad. I knew I should have stayed quiet.

'Girl, we all get those feelings,' says Melody. 'I can't believe you're only just having them.'

Air flows through my nostrils like a pressure cooker letting off steam. 'You do?'

'Course we do,' says Darla with a sad smile. I feel awful. Here's me moaning, wishing I could have a different life and here's Darla wishing for her old one back. She sees my look and smiles. 'Everyone's life is different, but we all wish for something or other we can't have.'

Melody takes a drink of coffee then says, 'What constitutes a good marriage anyway? Is it staying power, passion, faithfulness?'

'I think its friendship and being kind to each other,' replies Darla.

We all turn to look at Daphne. 'What! I'm the expert now?'

'Three marriages,' says Darla holding up three fingers.

'I think all that proves is that I don't know what I'm looking for.'

'But you must have picked up some knowledge along the way,' I add.

Daphne pulls a thoughtful face and chews her lip. 'I'm probably going to shock you all now, but I don't think I know what I'm looking for.'

I'm sitting perfectly still and upright in my seat.

'I keep thinking I've found love. The beginnings are always so exciting,' she laughs. 'Lots of sex, romance, playfulness. Then as time ticks by everything seems to fizzle out for me. They stop buying flowers, I stop buying sexy lingerie, and eventually we just stop talking to each other. It's at that point that I know it's over. I mean, Rose, what on earth do you still talk about after forty years?'

'Just everyday stuff: the garden, what's in the news, how the kids are getting on, that kind of thing. Nothing exciting I'm sorry to say.'

'But you're still together,' says Darla, like that's everything, and I guess maybe that would be her perspective.

'We are, and we're best friends. I don't suppose we would be normal if we went our entire lives without falling out every now and again.'

'No, you wouldn't,' laughs Daphne.

'Would any of you ever cheat, if the opportunity presented itself to you?'

'No!' says Darla with quite some defiance.

'No,' says Melody, 'at least I don't think so.'

'Yes!' says Daphne, and we all laugh.

'Why?' I ask her.

'Life is short is the simple answer. I want to embrace and experience it as much as possible. I wouldn't want to hurt my husband, but if I thought the relationship was going nowhere I wouldn't hesitate to have an affair.'

'Wouldn't you feel guilty?'

She shrugs. 'Possibly, but you know men have been cheating on women since time began, it's kind of accepted.'

'It doesn't make it right,' says Darla.

'OK, let me frame it like this… if my husband was attentive, talkative and generally wanting to spend time with me, cheating on him wouldn't even cross my mind. Why would I need to cheat if he was fulfilling all my needs and I his? It is neglectful husbands who risk their wives cheating on them.'

It is indeed, oh it is indeed.

'What about you?' asks Melody, 'would you cheat?'

Everyone is looking at me. I hope I'm not going red, although I feel a measure of heat rising. 'No, of course not, I've got too much to lose.'

'That's one way of looking at it,' says Melody, 'but I would have thought your answer would have been you love him too much.'

I smile and lift my cup. I want out of this conversation. After I've gulped the last of my coffee down, I turn to Daphne. 'I see Laura's posting nudes on Facebook again.'

'Oh, that daughter of mine, she's so artistic. Don't you think they're tastefully done? Being at Art College has really brought her out of herself.'

Diverted! I listen intently and keep my eyes on Daphne's face because I'm totally aware that Melody is staring at me and not looking away.

Jealousy

I NEED TO RUN SOME ERRANDS and go to the bank to transfer some money from our savings to our day to day account which is getting low. The weather is still unnaturally hot and I'm wearing a thin cotton frock and sandals. I've pinned my grey hair up in a messy bun, just to keep it off my neck. There's nowhere to park outside the bank, so I pull into a spot a distance away and grumble to myself that I need to walk so far.

I've been walking with my head down, pavement gazing, but I have to look up as someone approaches. I give the old woman a hello smile and pass by, and that's when I see Joe. At first my heart lunges in delight, but very quickly I stop walking in shock. Someone behind me bumps into me.

'So sorry,' I say stepping to the side. The man tuts but goes on his way. My gaze jumps back to Joe, who is standing outside the bank.

Talking to a woman.

My heart pounds.

A tall girl, with a horsey laugh, a mop of ginger hair and freckle-speckled cheeks, keeps touching Joe's arm. He laughs at something she says. From my toes to my temple creeps a fit of irrational jealousy. I want to slap her and send her on her way.

Where has this 'demonic' character in me sprung from?

Joe's mine. All mine.

The trouble is... he isn't really, and he never will be. I should be happy he's found someone else. I'll let him go. I'll be strong. I turn on my heels and rush back to the car before he spots me.

Who is she? Why did she keep touching him? Why didn't Joe tell her to stop? Oh damn, I feel sick. I'm panting by the time I get back in the car. I want to cry, but I tell myself off. Get a grip woman! After a couple of minutes in the cool of the car's air conditioning I've calmed down. She could be anyone. Just because I don't know her doesn't mean she hasn't been Joe's friend for years. She could be gay, oh God please let her be gay! She's far too beautiful to just be a friend.

I take deep calming breaths and continue to tell myself off. Is this what love does, makes you irrational? I don't remember ever being jealous of my husband's female friends. He's definitely never been jealous of my male friends either. I used to think it was because we trusted each other, now I have a sneaky suspicion it wasn't that at all.

I can't stand the thought of Joe being with another woman, I feel physically sick at just the thought, goodness knows what I'd be like if he was actually with someone. I shake my head. I don't even want to imagine what it would be like.

When I'm calm I head back to the bank. Joe and the redhead are nowhere to be seen. I'm both happy and worried. Maybe they've gone back to his flat for sex. I have to grab the wall to stop myself from falling over.

'Are you alright?' asks a kindly customer on their way out.

'Yes, thank you. I'm fine, thank you.'

The woman doesn't seem convinced but she nods and leaves me to my wobble.

'Oh Joe, I can't lose you, I can't.'

I CAN'T SLEEP. An image of Joe kissing the redhead swims before my face all night long. I waver between fits of jealous anger and an acceptance that he needs to move on and this is for the best.

By the morning I'm shattered, more tired than when I went to bed. I've also made my mind up to go around and confront him this evening when he gets home from work. It's a Wednesday which is one of Felicity's nights to have Freddie so I know Joe will be on his own – well hopefully!

As the day progresses I come to the decision that Joe will think me a crazy person if I just turn up and demand to know if he's seeing someone. Needing an excuse to visit I decide to buy Freddie a birthday present.

'That's a bit extravagant isn't it,' says Harvey when I tell him I'm popping around to Joe's.

'As it happens, no, it was on sale, I got it for half price.'

'I can't remember you buying Freddie birthday presents before.' He's snapping the words and his face is red. He pierces me with his cold stare.

'I've bought him a present for his birthday every year since he was born, which shows what little attention you ever pay me!' I didn't mean to bark back, guilt is probably causing the rush of anger that swims inside me.

Harvey raises his eyebrows at me and puts down his newspaper. I don't want to delay going to Joe's, but I can't walk out on this, I need to patch it up quickly.

'Sorry, I didn't mean that. You probably never noticed because normally I do a pile of shopping for presents in one go and then put them in the back of the cupboard for when they're needed.'

'But not this time.' He nods at the guitar in my hand.

'No, I admit this was a spur-of-the-moment kind of decision, I just saw it and knew Freddie would love it. You don't begrudge the money do you?'

Bring it back to money. He can never argue with how much I spend because compared to him I spend so little. Mean of me, but I want out of here.

'No of course not, I'm sure he'll love it.'

I go over and kiss him on the forehead. 'I won't be long.'

'Drive carefully.'

'I will.'

My heart is pounding by the time I get in the car. I don't like this new me who finds lying so easy.

Joe and I agreed at the beginning of this relationship that we absolutely mustn't text or message each other, nothing should be done that might give cause for suspicion. I'll use that as my excuse for not telling him that I'm coming over.

Part of me is going over all the things I will say to him if I knock at his door and find 'freckles' there.

Anger seethes in my chest, it's hot and uncomfortable. I need Joe's reassurance he hasn't got a new girlfriend to cool it down.

I knock. Thud-thud goes my heart. I wait. It feels like an eternity. Is he hiding a woman away in his bedroom so I won't see her? I'm being ridiculous of course; he doesn't even know it's me at the door.

'Rose?'

He's pleasantly surprised. Oh thank God, he can't have anyone here.

'I've bought Freddie a birthday present.' I lift up the small guitar and a flash of *Dirty Dancing* comes to mind where Baby (ridiculous name) tells Johnny she's carried a watermelon. Heat creeps into my cheeks.

'Come in.'

I get the impression he's laughing at me. 'You know I don't have Freddie until Saturday afternoon this week?'

'Oh, I wasn't sure. Anyway it's here now, for when he comes.'

'But you could have brought it around on Saturday morning, unless you're not planning on coming over?'

'I am.'

'Good, don't know what I would do without our Saturday mornings.' He winks at me. It causes me to properly smile for the first time since spotting him outside the bank.

'I thought you might enjoy teaching Freddie how to play.'

'Actually, I've just recently started teaching him. Although now he has his own guitar he'll probably enjoy it much more, holding mine was a bit difficult for him.'

I flush with pleasure, so happy that I got the right gift.

'You should stay on Saturday, give him the present yourself when he arrives.'

'I can't do that.'

Joe lets out a heavy sigh. 'Why not? You don't have to be naked and in my bed to be here, you could just act normal and be the friend you've always been to us.'

Ouch Joe, sometimes you cut deep. What is it with the men in my life right now? Why are they getting irritated with me?

He's right of course, I should be acting normal.

'I think pretending there is nothing going on between us is a bit too hard for me right now. I'll try to improve. I wouldn't want Freddie thinking I don't like him anymore.'

Joe wraps his arms around me. I love his arms. I love this feeling.

'He won't think that, but I have a sneaky feeling he's going to be so excited he's going to want to come and see you and say thank you himself. That will be OK won't it?'

'Yes, of course. In fact I'll let everyone know you're coming over Saturday afternoon and see if they fancy giving him a second birthday tea.'

'You sure?'

'Absolutely.' I can be normal. I can be normal. I can be normal.

'Give us a kiss!'

OK, with Joe's lips on me I don't think I can be normal.

When Joe starts getting a bit too amorous I push away. 'I can't stay, he knows I'm here.'

'Are you playing with fire, Rose?'

'I hope not.' And then from nowhere, well maybe from the depths of my insecurities I fire a question at him, 'Are you seeing someone else?' I suck my breath in through my nose. I didn't mean to say that. He's going to think me crazy.

He half laughs. 'No... why would you think that?'

I can't think fast enough, always a problem of mine, so I opt for the truth. 'I saw you outside the bank yesterday. You were with someone.'

He scrunches his face for a moment and I can tell he's recalling his movements. 'You mean Josephine?'

'I don't know who she is. She's beautiful though, red hair and freckles, tall and slim. Young.' Everything I'm not and more.

Joe's looking at me. It's dawning on him that I'm jealous, his eyes are laughing. Oh no, he's going to laugh at me. He roars, proper head back, tummy rolling, 'I find this so funny' kind of laugh.

I pick up my bag, it's time to go.

'Rose,' he cries coming out of his hysterics. He pulls me into his arms again and starts smothering me with kisses. I begin to melt. When he's kissed me enough that the tension has fallen off my shoulders he leans back and grins at me. 'God but I *love* that you're jealous.'

'I never said I was jealous!'

'Oh yes you did, my little firecracker. I love it, Rose. It means you love me more than you'll ever say in words. You just made me the happiest man on Earth!'

'Oh give over,' I playfully slap his arms off me. 'I've got to get home.'

'Rose loves me, Rose loves me,' he calls after me as I go down the stairs.

'Shut up, Joe!' I bark back at him.

He leans on the balcony of the flat and calls out over the car park. 'Rose loves me, Rose loves me.'

I wave a fist at him and drive away.

Forbidden Fruit

I DON'T THINK THIS WAS A GOOD IDEA. Everyone is here, the grandchildren are playing in the paddling pool, and Freddie is enjoying being the center of attention. He's a bright-eyed mischievous young man, a mini Joe.

Harvey is being a grump and we've frowned at each other several times. I'm trying to be 'normal' but a harder task would be difficult to find! Gemma just made a comment about my makeup and I nearly had a fit! I've only put on a little eye-shadow, mascara and lipstick, not a big deal! My dress is new, but I'm losing weight and need something that fits me better, no big deal! I don't know why she made such a fuss commenting on how lovely and glowing I am. I don't know why Harvey took it so badly and went storming off.

'You look amazing,' Joe whispers in my ear and I realize my mistake. I don't normally look *amazing* for children's parties, or adult ones for that matter. Harvey is going to be wondering what's going on.

I give Joe a slight glare and move away from him. I can't be normal when he's too close.

'Mum you look a million dollars,' says Jake giving me a hug.

'It was in a sale,' I blurt, like I need to defend why I'm wearing a new dress.

'It was a good buy. The dark shade of green illuminates the green in your eyes. You look beautiful.'

My heart fills with love and appreciation for my children. I also try to recall the last time Harvey paid me a compliment and I can't remember it. I look at Jake and smile, standing slightly taller than I had a moment ago. Why shouldn't I wear a little make-up and buy a new dress?

The afternoon party doesn't last long. I learn a quick-step that keeps me moving out of Joe's vicinity. That's not possible when he asks me if we can light the candles in front of everyone. Of course I have to say yes.

He leans into me by the kitchen table and hisses, 'If you keep walking away when I approach you everyone will cotton on to the fact that something is wrong. Just breathe, relax and act normal.'

'It's too hard!'

I spin around and head out of the kitchen to round everyone up to sing happy birthday.

Joe is holding the cake in front of Freddie; his whole countenance is one of love. My heart melts. Joe glances at me briefly as Freddie blows out the candles. His love for me pours from him and I turn away.

HARVEY HAS GONE AWAY for the weekend and Felicity has taken Freddie to Alton Towers for the weekend... we grab the opportunity and plan a night together. I'm nervous, more jittery than our first time together. I think it's the naughtiness of it. The forbidden adding a certain glisten on our immoral rendezvous.

We've driven to Wales and I don't know if I'm more nervous or excited. We've only booked a roadside motel, nothing fancy. But from its location we can easily drive to Snowdonia and visit Betws-y-Coed, a place I love and haven't visited for years.

We walk for a few hours enjoying the beauty of the mountains and rivers. Then we go to a pub within walking distance of the motel and have dinner. I'm more on edge than I thought I would be as I can't shift the fear that someone we know might spot us.

Joe is more relaxed than me, I can't help thinking he would be secretly happy if we got caught out. We have a few glasses of a rich, fruity, Portuguese red wine. It goes to my head pretty quickly. I can't eat much; I'm consumed with wondering what it will be like to spend an entire night in Joe's strong arms.

Back in the room we fall upon each other the way that only people in love can do. Our eye contact is intense and stays with us throughout. We can't stop kissing and during everything we cling to each other. Our touches are gentle and affectionate and there's no rush, everything we do makes us feel good. All my life I have been dreaming of this type of connection. I didn't know how good it could be. I could weep that I've been married for forty years and never had this once.

Joe settles over me with ease and precision, as if we'd done this a thousand times before. Home – returned to after a long and arduous voyage. Home – where scents of pine and honeysuckle welcome you back. Home, a place of safety and comfort, and a place you never want to leave again. Home.

Joe is my home.

Our lovemaking causes tears to flow; they're of wonder and joy. His touches evoke feelings of life within me, causing rivers to flow, refreshing my almost dead body. I am Pinocchio and my dream has come true.

THE PALE LIGHT OF DAWN creeps through the gap in the curtains; its fingers illuminate Joe with an ethereal glow. His honey-brown eyes watch me. His soul is laid bare and I see him! The sunrise rips back his layers – so many layers.

Why have I never seen him before?

I'm not the only one who camouflages myself. Joe is a master chameleon, changing his persona to fit the moment. Here, now, in the promise of a new day, I see his vulnerability. He is naked, both in flesh and spirit.

Every motherly instinct floods to the surface. I want to protect him, care for him, ensure his happiness.

'Oh, Joe!'

As we move together once more, both frantic and tender, our flesh is so close that no air can pass between us. His kisses are giving as he pours himself into me. He's melting my heart. His touch draws me out of myself until every part of me is being offered to him.

When thoughts begin to return and our bodies clasp desperately to each other, I speculate over the conundrum of my blindness. How is it that I have never really looked before? I did see his needs as a boy, food, family life, a safe place to come. I saw his actions, the games and fights. I even heard his words. But until this moment I'd never actually seen *him*. How did I miss his passion, and his love of life?

Love Me

WHATEVER I HAVE WITH JOE is both wonderful and transient. Deep inside I know all the sensations he evokes within me will have no chance against the love I have for these people. I'm sure he knows it too, which is what makes him so desperate to win me.

'Nana, Nana.' Chloe runs across the kitchen tiles in her bare feet. Her blonde curls bouncing off her shoulders.

I smile and bend down to her height. 'What is it, my little princess?'

'Oliver wants a cookie.' She's twirling on her toes and pulling a mouth that tells me it's Chloe that wants a biscuit really.

'If you both eat lots of your dinner, you can have cookies afterwards.'

'Okaaay.' She's disappointed but bounces off to play for the last ten minutes before we sit down.

'You OK, Mum?'

'Yes thanks Luke, do you want to help me get everything on the table?'

'Sure.'

'Need a hand?' ask Eleanor, Luke's wife.

'We got it love, just keep an eye on the kids, Chloe's hovering around Dad's sweet tin.'

'Is she?' Eleanor spins quickly and heads back into the front room.

Luke and I share secret smiles. Chloe and Oliver are not allowed sweets, rots the teeth don't you know, but Luke and I have a pact which means he brings sweets around here and puts them in the tin in the front room. We tell Eleanor they're Harvey's but in truth they're for the grandkids when the parents aren't looking. I just get them to clean their teeth afterwards.

Thursday night is family night, I'm not sure how the tradition started but we all love it. Mostly, like today, I do a roast. Sometimes in summer we have something cooler with less work to make, but today it's roast beef with all the trimmings. Eleanor is a vegetarian (and hugely trying to encourage their children and Luke in that regard) so there is an asparagus and goat cheese tart for her, which she says she loves. I don't think she'll ever persuade Luke to give up his meat but they've come to an agreement that he only eats meat four times a week. I think it's a bit pushy but he seems happy so I don't interfere.

'Ready,' I call placing the Yorkshire puddings in the middle of the table. The family flood in chatting away. Everyone's here, including Penny, I've got to give credit to Jake for being so forgiving.

Harvey carves the beef and everyone passes their plates to him. Oliver is in the high chair whacking it with his plastic spoon while shoving carrots in his mouth.

'Ethan's got some news,' says Gemma once food has been dished out.

'What's that?' asks Luke.

'I've got the promotion I was after,' Ethan declares with a lot of pride. And so he should, we know a lot of people applied for the position. We all smile and congratulate him. My heartbeat has quickened slightly because I know the new post is in North Manchester and there's a good chance if he likes the job that they will move house so he can be nearer to work. I offer my congratulations, it's a huge pay rise and I know he deserves it, I just hope they can't see that behind my smile I'm sad. The distance will mean that we see each other less than now. I've always been delighted that all three of our children stayed so close to home, but this promises to be the beginning of the end to that.

I take a long breath and smile as Gemma tells us all the new details about the job. They have their own lives to live, they can't hold back because of me.

'Penny's applied for a new job too,' says Jake.

My head snaps up and I look at her. She's looking straight back at me when she speaks. She's giving me the details because besides Jake I'm the only one who knows of her transgression; because at the last minute Jake decided he didn't want anyone else to know. I think this is the first family secret that I have kept from my husband, but it's Jake's choice.

'I've applied for an accounts job in a firm just down the road, if I get it, it will mean only ten minutes travel to work instead of forty-five, I think it will be great.'

Yes, and get you away from the man you cheated with. 'I think that's a good move,' I smile at her. She looks shy. I'm overcome with empathy for her. I'm sinning in a far worse way than she did and if Jake can forgive her then so can I.

I lean across the table and squeeze her hand. I notice her eyes fill up and remove my hand; she won't want to cry in front of everyone.

The family are talking, exchanging their news and passing comments on current events. It's only towards the end of the meal that it dawns on me that Harvey has been unusually quiet.

I glance at him when we start clearing up, he offers me a smile, but somehow I know it's false and I wonder what's going on.

He snapped at me this morning when I asked him if he wanted to go to the pictures. He told me the cinema was too expensive and a waste of money, and that I should wait for them to appear on Netflix or Amazon. I barked back about all the money he's spent on golf and he'd gone quiet. All this bickering is out of character for both of us and has given me a sense of unease.

I'll have to find the right moment and have a talk with him and find out what's eating him. But for now I just want to enjoy the family.

I TRY TO TALK TO HARVEY before he goes out for golf, but he is still bad tempered and keeps cutting me off. By the time he leaves I am rather irritated with him.

For a moment it makes me want to pack my bags and leave. I clean up the house and put a lamb casserole in the slow cooker, and then I go for a shower. Under the water I try and work out what's bothering him, a slight panic that he might know about me and Joe eats at me, but obviously he can't know about us otherwise he would be more than a little irritable, he'd be screaming at me to leave!

In a way I'm glad he's not being nice, it makes me feel less guilty about going to see Joe.

'YOU'RE LATE,' says Joe when I arrive.

'I know, sorry, I just needed to get some things done.'

'You look tired.'

'I didn't sleep much last night.' I tossed and turned most of the night worrying about what could be wrong with my husband, but I can't tell Joe that.

'Cup of tea?'

'Just some water please.'

We curl up on the sofa and chat about our week. We swap news and listen intently to each other. We talk over all our plans for next week when we'll be flying to Santorini. I still can't believe it.

'And everyone accepts that you want a week on your own?'

'Yes, I was quite surprised that the kids even thought it was a good idea! They've always said it isn't fair that their dad gets to go on several holidays a year and I never go anywhere on my own.'

'And *he* was OK?'

'Yes, he surprised me. He told me to order myself five hundred Euros and to have a good time, I nearly fell over.'

Joe's arms tighten around me. 'The man is a fool, I'd never let you go off on your own. I'd want to go with you, and honestly I'd be too afraid some tall dark stranger would sweep you off your feet!'

'I guess that's it isn't it, he just doesn't think anyone will find me attractive anymore.'

'Hey, less of that.' Joe kisses me and soon we're in the bedroom.

I must have dozed because I wake with a start.

'It's OK, you're not late.' Joe smiles at me and my heart melts. He's got dressed, worn jeans and an unbuttoned shirt. His shoulder-length curly brown hair cascades around his face. He's got an after-sex glow about him, I could eat him.

'What you doing?'

He's pulled a kitchen chair into the bedroom and has his guitar on his lap. 'From the moment you fell asleep a song came into my head and won't go away. I want to sing it to you.'

He drops his gaze as his fingers begin to strum the guitar. He hums and flicks his hair off his face. He starts quietly but it's building, getting louder and louder, and then he drops to quiet and soft. He doesn't have the best voice in the world, but it's full of character and easy to listen to.

The first words of the song come out of him no louder than a whisper, but his heart flows into his mouth when he sings the chorus…

> *If I just lay here*
> *Would you lie with me and just forget the world?*

He loses himself in the song. The words pour from him and he means every single one of them.

> *Show me a garden that's bursting into life (Snow Patrol, Chasing Cars, 2006)*

Tears stream unchecked over my cheeks, but I'm smiling.

It's like all my life I've been waiting for a man to serenade me. My heart has cracked open and is leaking out loneliness, while Joe's love slips inside. It's beautiful, everything is beautiful. Both the song and Joe are perfect. This is who I am; a woman who gets serenaded – a woman who is loved and loves in return.

I have beautiful moments, memories I store in my head and in photographs: My wedding day, the births of my children, playing games with them when they were little; talking around the dinner table for hours as they grew up. A family barbeque on the beach at sunset. The sun on my Dad's face on the last time I was able to take him out for a day trip. Memories, precious and wonderful, the building blocks of my life. The purpose for my being. I love them all, they complete me, make me whole.

But this… this breaks down that whole and takes me to a place of rawness. A place where feeling replaces memory. I know I will never have this again but if I store this up in my treasure chest of memories, it will eat me alive and destroy me. So I will forget to hang on to it, I won't force a picture of it into my mind. Instead I will live it, experience it, and then let it go.

When he finishes, Joe crawls over the bed covers to me. He kisses my tears. We fall into each other, hungry.

He devours me.

I moan.

He consumes.

I surrender.

I shudder as I offer my very core to this man who sees me.

We lie together.

Tangled.

Unmoving.

Breathing heavy.

I want to stay here forever. I've given all I am. This is what I want.

Joe is what I want.

'You scare me, Rose.'

I shudder, that had been my thought such a short while ago. I await his explanation both terrified and thrilled.

'I think a man only properly loves once in his life. He finds a woman who awakens him. She ignites his fire, burns down his walls of self-preservation, until his naked soul is laid bare before her. A bit like a dog that rolls onto his back revealing its belly to his master.'

'You do have a *very* nice belly!'

'A dog's stomach is its weakest part, if offered to the wrong person or creature it could mean its death. When a man offers his innermost self it is only to a woman who he hopes will be his life partner. I'm looking for my soul mate and I'm scared that's you, because I sense you're never going to pick me.'

'You should let me go then.'

'You don't know how many times over the years I've wanted to touch your hair. To touch you. I can't believe you're here. Shall I tell you how I know I love you?'

I nod.

'My right shoulder has been a cause of pain since I hurt it playing football when I was teenager. At night pain causes me to toss and turn. Yet when we were in Wales and you fell asleep curled on my chest under my right arm, I couldn't move you. Pain shot through me but I would rather have that pain and hold you than not have you in my arms.'

I guess once a woman becomes a mother she will carry maternal instincts for the rest of her life; I need to love and protect him. I take his hand and kiss his palm trying to calm the storm I see brewing in him. I kiss his wrist, one then the other. His chest rises and falls rapidly, too fast.

'Breathe Joe, breathe.'

I place my hand on his chest. His heart plays a beat against my palm. Oh my poor love.

'Should I go?'

He wraps his arms around me, melding us together. He's shaking, and I sense his emotions are like a flood against a dam. 'No, for as long as I can love you, I will, just love me back, Rose. Love me a little, please.'

I love him then with all my might. I try to bring him happiness by my touches and kisses.

'I always wondered what you would feel like, naked in my arms, your hips under mine.'

'Are you disappointed? I mean that would be totally understandable. I'm old for a start, and dreams are rarely as spectacular as we imagine them to be.'

'Rose, will you shut up,' he half laughs. 'Let me enjoy my fantasy come reality.'

'Oh! OK.'

He spins me over onto my back and lowers himself over me, kissing me tenderly. As his hands roam I'm shocked at how loud my moans are. I raise my hips. I have come to appreciate the coming together of lovers and my body is longing for fulfillment.

When he enters me I explode with a million sensations. I can't think anymore. I'm lost. This time is over too quickly for me, I hadn't reached that magical pinnacle. We're both releasing tears. I cry because any moment in Joe's arms is wonderful and beautiful, and because I never thought I would be loved like this.

I want to know why Joe is crying but I can't bring myself to ask him. I assume it's because he knows this love is doomed.

Love feels like when you're at a wedding and you're not quite ready to dance but then *Dancing Queen* comes on and it's all over.

The Holiday

I WAVE GOODBYE TO JAKE until his car is out of sight. My heart's beating alarmingly fast, I'm worried I'm going to keel over. Guilt or excitement? Your guess is as good as mine. A deep breath, an attempt at composure, and then I tilt my case and strike a most determined step into terminal two.

Who would believe that Manchester airport could be heaving with thousands of people at 3.30 am? Not me. How will I find him?

'Rose.'

Of course he'd find me!

'This way.'

No kiss or even an embrace. Too many people and things that could bring our world tumbling down.

We queue. Our conversation is muted, almost like strangers. All I want to do is crush him in a hug. Is he as excited as I am? We approach the desk together and ask to be seated next to each other.

'There are only seats available at the back of the plane,' she smiles apologetically.

'No problem,' answers Joe.

Suitcases gone. I'm going on holiday! A wickedly, naughty holiday. I've never been to Santorini before. I've never had an affair before! I should be feeling guilty but I'm just too excited.

Security is a nightmare. I've put my mask on. Three lanes over a little boy is coughing his poor little guts out. It sounds like he's got croup. Several lines behind us a woman is barking loud dry coughs. Shouldn't they have stayed at home? Covid's on the rise again. 1.2 million people have it in England at the moment apparently. I sincerely hope none of them are here with us. Why aren't more people wearing masks? Am I just a paranoid nutter? What if someone we know sees us? I feel sick. Too many people. Too close.

'Rose?'

I snap my eyes upwards.

'It's OK. Everything is OK.'

I think I love you! Half a smile tugs at my lips. I hope it convinces him that I'm alright.

The queue's moving. I turn forward again and take five steps to catch up before coming to a halt again. Some things about holidays are just not any fun. Joe takes five steps, only his strides are longer than mine and now he's breathing down my neck. It's warm and spicy and deliciously wrong. We don't hang around duty-free; we head straight for the bar. I need coffee, we buy rum and coke instead.

'It'll calm your nerves.'

'I hope so because right now I'm wondering what the protocol is for leaving an airport once you've cleared security.'

'Gin rummy?'

'You want to play cards now?'

'Yes.'

The man's a genius. Two drinks and four games of rummy later I'm laughing and relaxed. I've still got half an eye on the crowd seeking familiar faces, but so far so good.

When I click the belt on I'm more excited than panicky. Joe leans over and gives me a smacker on my lips that sends thrills all over me. He takes hold of my hand like he's done it a million times before. I like it. I like it a lot.

Wow, it's so hot! We follow instructions and make our way to the tour company coach. We're the last to be dropped off. The ride has been hairy to say the least. At a couple of spots the road is so close to the cliff edge I think we're going to go over. Our driver seems unfazed by the number of cars that beep at him or the fists that wave at him out of car windows. I keep closing my eyes. The views are lost on me as I grip Joe's hand in fear. He can't stop chuckling at me, but I notice he isn't looking out of the window either.

Our hotel is in the lower price range. Guilt would only allow me to spend so much from our joint bank account. I should be spending thousands to match my hubby's holiday allowance, but I can't. He's the one who worked all those years to live this comfy retired life, I can't help but still think of it as his money. He always tells me it's our money, and he certainly never checks with me when he forks out his fortune in golf clubs and memberships. My writing, reading and knitting hobbies don't even make up five percent of what he spends. I've paid for the room. Joe is going to fork out for our meals. It seems like a fair trade.

The room is large and clean, although the promised sea view is only a triangle between distant trees; the rest is a dusty car park. Our bathroom smells and the walls are dotted with mold, I'm not impressed. I want to cry. I don't do mildew. I'm going to have to find a shop and buy some bleach. I read an article once on the corruption of the spores that come off mold and how they can damage your lungs. It's put me on the edge of fear ever since.

Inbred politeness means I don't say anything to the lady who has shown us to our room. 'Thank you,' I smile at her.

As soon as she has gone I groan. 'Oh, it's awful! I'm sorry I picked such a place. And there's no kettle, how are we going to have a cuppa in the mornings?' Even I can hear the high-pitched tone of my voice, pure panic attack level.

Joe's in front of me straight away. His beautiful eyes are sparkling with mischief and merriment. He cups my face with his hands. I close my eyes. His lips flutter over mine. His kiss is soft, reassuring. I relax.

'Better?' He asks five minutes later.

'Umm-hum.'

'Let's unpack and then go for a walk.'

I could kiss him again – in all the places that would drive him crazy, because I love that he knows I can't jump straight between the sheets. We get the giggles unpacking. Sharing secret smiles as we hang dresses and shirts, and put toiletries in the bathroom. We're here. We're really here! Maybe this wasn't such a crazy idea after all.

We head off to explore. Hand-in-hand we stroll along the beach road that's largely covered with a smattering of black, gritty sand. We dodge cars, trikes and motorbikes.

Although the sand is heavily pebbled, (and in my opinion an extremely large litter tray for the hundreds of cats that live here) I want to paddle, so we head towards the sea. The water is refreshingly cold and I can't wait until tomorrow when we can go for a swim.

By the time I've clocked the fifth person giving us a long stare, I realize our age difference is too vast to pretend it doesn't exist or that people won't notice. We might not notice our age gap anymore, but other people sure do. I move closer to Joe and, always hyper-sensitive to my mood, he wraps an arm around me.

'Don't mind them.'

'But they're staring.'

'So?'

'It reminds me this is nuts. I feel uncomfortable.'

'They're only jealous.'

'Jealous?'

'Yep, not every woman can find themselves a handsome hunk like me. And hey, I can't help it if my stunning physiognomy draws attention!'

I'm laughing. 'You nutter.'

'You know it's me they're jealous of, right?'

I glance up with a raised eyebrow.

'They're all wondering how a gnome like me was able to catch a beauty like you.'

'Joe! You're not ugly, far from it.'

'That's sweet of you to say, but I know what I am and accept it. This is the face I was born with and not a lot I can do about it.'

'I love your face.'

'I'd rather you love me.'

There, on the beach, for all to see Joe takes me in his arms and gives me a good old-fashioned snog. I'm a teenager again. I don't care about the world, all I want is this.

By the time we're walking back to the hotel, I don't care about the stares anymore.

The melodic crash of waves against the black sand, the music streaming from every restaurant and bar, the periodic roar of car engines, all blend together and create an orchestra of happiness.

We're happy and relaxed. We're holding hands in public. My cup overflows.

We stop for cocktails. We only planned on one, but four drinks later we're laughing with the waiter and singing along to the ghetto-blasting music.

At a certain point my eyes must betray me. Joe gives a nod and declares, 'Right, time to go.'

Stars twinkle, the moon rises and the sea continues its eternal dance. Hardly changing throughout time these immortal instruments observe the feeble attempts of humans. Maybe they smile, maybe they frown. For we stumble through life searching for love's perfection, not always in the right places. I wonder what they think of me and Joe.

We enter the room that earlier had put so much fear in my heart I'd thought God might strike me dead. Now I look at the space before us in a new light. It is a vessel of exploration in which we can relax and enjoy being together. It is a gift I will not reject.

In between kisses we undress. Romantically Joe guides me to bed and we lie down.

'Blooming heck! The mattress is like a piece of wood. I'll never be able to sleep on this!'

'Good, because I don't expect we'll get much time for sleep.'

'Oh!'

Oh indeed! We did sleep though, after we enjoyed the pleasures of lovemaking. We slept for nearly eleven hours! All my worries that my snoring and passing wind would send him running for the hills has been for naught, for I don't think there ever was a man who slept so peaceful and totally unaware of what was happening right beside him!

BY THE TIME WE'D PLAYED and showered we'd missed breakfast. With loud grumbling stomachs, we set off along the road in search of sustenance. We end up in a pancake bar. I pick waffles, ice cream and chocolate sauce, not the healthiest but most definitely satisfying.

We do the things of lovers eternal: he smears chocolate sauce on my nose and kisses it off. I pinch his last piece of bacon by getting him to turn around. We giggle. Just here and right now we are free people, indulging ourselves and blocking out the real world.

We swim and neck in the sea until we're overcome with passion and have to rush back to our room, dripping wet and laughing. We make the most of our time. I'm acutely aware that every moment we have is stolen and precious. Hours are lost as we talk and talk and talk. Unraveling our past we share our highlights and offer comfort to each other when we touch upon the sad.

We stay away from our shared memories, they involve my family and at the moment neither of us is brave enough to touch on the elephant in the room. We stubbornly refuse to talk about the future. This week is about the here and now… and us, just us. The fact that we don't have a future is a dark veil of reality that keeps my feet on solid ground, and stops me from fantasizing about a life that will never ever be.

'Is everything alright with your bathroom?' asks a concerned cleaner early in the morning on our third day. Her face is a picture of worry and confusion.

My cheeks burn with intense heat, 'Yes thank you, everything is fine.' I grin like a crazy Cheshire cat and leg it. How can I explain to the ultra-pleasant staff member that pooping in your room and discarding tissue into a shared bin is *not* my type of romantic action? I've been visiting the public toilets by the swimming pool to save my embarrassment. If I wrote a travel blog I'd say Santorini is a wonderful romantic island if you've been married for years, but maybe not ideal if you're embarking on a brand new romantic relationship. I make a note for future holidays to check if the country allows you to drop paper down the toilet!

Joe thinks it's hysterical that I go to the public toilet, men! I'd be happier if he'd politely ignore my clandestine dawn escapades!

Catching the bus to Fira costs €2.20. We jump aboard and head off for the capital. At first I don't like how busy it is. I've gotten used to the quiet, sleepy Perissa Bay. The shops here are packed and expensive but full of lovely things. I purchase pretty, hand-painted bowls that will be perfect for things like peanuts. I get the grandchildren presents and a bottle of ouzo for Harvey. I see a bracelet I fall in love with. A silver and semi-precious stone-studded one, it is delicate and ultra-pretty, but I'm already consumed with guilt for spending money on the holiday, so after humming and hawing for a few minutes I put it back on the shelf.

For lunch we go into one of the many cliff-top restaurants. Iriana Café offers us spectacular views of the Aegean Sea and distant isles, it is quite breathtaking. Joe protests when I make a beeline straight for an empty table next to the small fence overlooking the cliff.

'Just look at this view,' I say, snapping away on my phone camera.

'No thanks,' he mutters and sticks his head behind the menu. I think he's messing at first, but by the time lunch arrives I know his fear of heights is real and the view horrifies him more than the crazy coach driver had frightened me. Needless to say we don't stay longer than we have to! The double-cappuccino is so nice I could drink three cups; I don't though because I'd have ended up as high as a kite. Trying to eat my Greek salad I get the giggles as Joe obstinately refuses to look to the left at the fantastic view.

After lunch we amble around the narrow streets and enjoy the atmosphere – minus the view. I'm finding the whole day incredibly romantic. I don't know why specifically, can't quite put my finger on it. We hold hands and often find ourselves gazing at each other, but we don't kiss much.

There's something exuberant about walking in the open and being unafraid. In a crowd of strangers, we can be ourselves. We're safe. Some glances come our way – I assume because of the age gap, but I attribute most to curiosity and like to think they're not judging us. Whatever their reason for looking it has no effect on me today. I'm just too happy to care, and that's all that matters right now. I've kept an Iriana Café business card, it's grey and gold. I plan to use it as a bookmark when I'm home. It will be a reminder of this perfect day.

THE WIND HAS PICKED UP and cooled the air. There are only two full days left before we fly back to reality. The approaching deadline has pulled a blanket of melancholy around us.

'Hey,' says Joe as we paddle in the sea. 'At least we'll always have *this* to remember.' I squeeze his hand. I can't answer. I feel like crying. 'Or,' he continues, 'we could just run away together. You and me Rose, against the world.'

'We'd miss our kids too much.'

'Maybe they'd come and visit us when they get over the shock?'

'Freddie is only twelve, you'd have to wait four years until he was old enough to choose to come and live with you. Felicity might be on talking terms with you, but she'd never let Freddie live somewhere else. So, Mr. Romantic you're speaking of impossible dreams. It's never going to happen.'

'I can't stop wishing though.'

'Nor me.' Those two little words reveal too much and I pinch my lips shut so I don't say anything else. We hold hands and stroll along the shore. 'If it helps you, try and imagine what I'm going to look like in ten years. I'll be seventy-four, wrinkles and floppy skin. It won't be pleasant!'

'Rose!' He stops and pulls me against him. 'You are, have always been, and will always remain beautiful to me. I see you, Rose. All of you. Inside and out. Trust me I'm not just saying this to butter you up, you're already tasty enough! I'm telling you God's honest truth. I love you, I have done for years, and I've a strong feeling that I will love you until the day I die.'

I tighten my grip around his waist and try to dispel the lump in my throat.

Joe kisses my head. 'You can break up with me if you must, like I sense you're going to do. But don't belittle what I feel, and don't lie and say it's because of our age.'

'OK.' The word is a squeak. I know it's not the answer he wants. He wants the lie. I can't give it. I can't fill his head with the promise of a life together. We can't even carry on seeing each other when we get back. That's something my muddled brain has already worked out. This thing, whatever it is, is too dangerous. We have to put the fire out… somehow.

'I love you, Rose.'

I bury my head in his chest and refuse to answer.

THE AIR CONDITIONER RATTLES reluctantly releasing a swish of air that's only a little cooler than the air outside. It is a right racket, sounding louder than a plane getting ready for takeoff. Joe and I are snuggled under the sheets; my head is on his chest. His arm lies protectively and possessively around me. Making love this morning was sad. He'd kissed my tears away. I hadn't been able to stop them. This thing is so bittersweet. I'm glad for it, but I also know it's time to have *the* talk we've both been dreading.

'Joe.'

Silence.

'When we get back.'

More silence.

'We have to stop.'

He's staring at the ceiling.

'Penny for your thoughts?'

'You know them already, Rose. Don't fish for final affirmations of my love. It doesn't become you.'

I feel like I've been slapped. 'I'm not! You're too harsh on me.'

'Am I now?'

'Yes!'

'What am I to you?'

I can't answer straight away. It's too complicated. After a while of silence I try to explain.

'I never realized I was lonely until you moved into my vision. I thought I was content, settled, my future mapped out before me. Then you took me in your arms and pulled me into a whirlwind of breathtaking life. From the moment you wrapped your arms around me I was undone. I yearned for you with such intensity it scared me to death.'

Joe takes hold of my hand. 'I think I've been waiting for you to look at me as a man since I was fifteen. I've dreamed of you, imagined you in my arms. Wondered what my flesh against your flesh would feel like. Would you thrill under my touch the way I imagined? Beyond that I dreamed of a life with you, a life I would make for us: A place where you would smile all day long – joyful smiles not sad ones like you often smile these days. I never thought it would happen. Yet here you are. I'm trying to enjoy every moment, but a shadow floats over everything we do. A storm so violent the weathermen would declare 'threat to life' that's what looms closer, and I'm terrified for both of us.'

'Maybe we'll get lucky and the storm will blow over?'

'I don't want it to blow over. I want the storm to hit and for you to decide which shelter you're going to run into.'

'Joe!'

'Just being honest.'

'All good things come to an end.'

Joe finally turns his gaze from the ceiling to my face. 'It doesn't have to. We could face the music and make a life for ourselves.'

I fully understand what it means to be ripped in two.

'What are we going to do, Rose? Are we going to let all of this go?' His questions are quiet, the still before the tempest. I can feel his turmoil, his rage that burns with intensity… towards me. His emotions are mounting, waking up like a sleeping lion.

I need to still the beast before it's unleashed. 'I care for you too much to allow you to tie yourself to an older woman. You're a free spirit, full of light and life. I wouldn't want to see that dim. I want you to find someone you can grow old with. An equal. Someone who will be able to love you forever, until you turn grey together.'

'I want to do that with you.'

'But I'm already old and grey. My time is running out, my light already pales. For goodness' sake, I get breathless from a flight of stairs. And my body is failing me. Arthritis cripples me some days. I don't want you to see that side of me.'

'You've been fine on this holiday.'

'No, I haven't. I've been in agony with all the walking and I'm popping pills every time your back is turned.'

'Oh, Rose. You should have said.'

'What, and show you how old I really am?' I laugh but it's a pain-filled, sorrowful sound.

Joe takes my hand in his, face full of concern.

'You deserve someone young,' I tell him.

'Trouble is… I love you. I have done for years. Now that you're with me I can't let you go.'

'But you must.'

'We fit together.'

I know we do. We fit into each other like two halves being connected becoming a whole. I need to tell him it's over but I don't want to spoil what's been a perfect holiday so I smile instead. 'We'll see.'

'You to me are the sun on a dull day. You glimmer through clouds and promise warmth.'

Something inside me is going crazy.

He carries on. 'I'm chasing that warmth because it makes me feel whole. I never even knew a part of me was missing until we kissed. I thought my infatuation with you stemmed from my boyhood fantasies. I didn't know it was flowing from a need to be complete.'

I roll my head and kiss his chest. It is all I can offer. I hope that he is finished, but he still has more to say.

'Little did I know that by being complete with you I was dooming myself to be broken and less of a man than I was before.'

'Oh, Joe!' I smother him with kisses: His chest, neck, face, and his lips that melt against mine. 'Joe. Joe.'

'It's OK, Rose, I understand.'

No more words, just a mix of pleasure and pain. Touching each other, smiling smiles that don't reach the eyes – where all sparkle has now diminished.

Love.

Not always rosy, yet always desired and chased.

Love.

Tentatively given, generously received.

Love.

Love with no words or labels. Just love.

That's what we have for each other in this moment. Let tomorrow rain down what it may.

⁂

THE NEXT DAY, we pack and say goodbye to the friendly staff and climb the steps onto the coach. We're returning home different. I know now that what I feel for Joe isn't just misguided appreciation for the fact that he wants me. Desires me. It isn't a last-ditch attempt to remain young. This is real. It's honest and it's true. It's also a love that binds us together in sin.

Love.

Love.

Love.

Unfortunately, love is never enough. Nor is it ever the whole picture.

My life is full of love, and I'm grateful, sincerely thankful for it. I know how lucky I am, how blessed beyond measure.

Only a few words pass between us all the way home. We grip hands, afraid to let go, locked in our separate torture. At customs, Joe kisses my cheek and I set off alone.

Jake picks me up. Joe and I had agreed earlier that Joe would linger in arrivals and grab a coffee, giving Jake and I time to leave before Joe exits the airport. Something is swirling inside me and I know that sadness has come to settle and stay a while.

Armageddon

Lost between the pages of a risqué book, I slip discreetly into a world of sexual fantasy. I switch the character in the book to Joe. He follows me with a panther-like pursuit, stalking me until I'm forced to acknowledge his presence. He pounces. He's forceful; his hands are everywhere creating magic upon my skin, filling me with passionate sensations. He murmurs words of seduction and love, tells me I'm beautiful, a lie I gladly accept. His hands slip between my thighs. I moan.

'You alright, Dear?'

'What?' I bolt upright with a guilty start, slamming my book shut.

'I heard you moan, are you OK?'

'Oh, it's just my back as normal, pretty awful, been giving me gyp all day.'

'Do you want me to get you some painkillers?'

Sweet man, he makes me blush, I feel ashamed. 'No, it's alright. I'd rather wait until bedtime then I'll take the extra strong ones to help me sleep.'

'If you're sure.'

I nod.

'Well I'm off out to see Charlie, he's having problems with his laptop, said I'd help him sort it out, you know how un-techie he is!'

'OK, see you later.'

Harvey looks at me with an expression I can't read, it's almost like he's trying to work out what's wrong with me. Well, I mean, moaning in the morning is maybe a bit too much, even for me.

'I'll be back before dinner.'

'OK.' I smile. I hope it doesn't look false.

When the front door shuts I sigh with relief and flop back on the sofa. I lift the book up and look at the cover; it's a muscular man without a shirt, very dishy. I've never read books like this in my life.

Am I changing, or is this the real me?

I put the book in my knitting bag, out of sight, and go into the kitchen. I need to do something else and get out of my head a bit. I decide on lamb curry, it takes me ages to make, although I always make a pot large enough to feed an army as I like to box up portions and stick them in the freezer for days when I want an easy meal.

The house has curry aromas wafting through it, even though all the windows are open, as are the patio doors. The fan is also on, helping to chase them away and to keep me cool in this particularly hot summer that doesn't seem to want to end even though October is only a few days away.

The doorbell rings and I hear the door open.

'Hellooo.'

I smile, it's Eleanor. 'Hi,' I yell, 'I'm in the kitchen.'

'I can tell,' she says coming in. 'It smells wonderful in here.'

We hug. Something in the hug lets me know that something's not quite right.

'You OK?' I ask.

'Sure am, I'm good actually. I just popped around to see how *you're* doing.'

'Oh you know me, nothing much happens, all is good.'

'Umm.'

Oh no, someone else who's questioning what's going on with me. Am I really acting so out of character?

'Coffee or wine?' I ask, hopefully deflecting her.

'Do you have rosé?'

'I do indeed. Why don't you grab the bottle and a couple of glasses and take them out on the patio. I just need five minutes to finish off here.'

'Sure.'

Adding the coriander to the pot I can't help but sigh. I like Eleanor, she's made Luke very happy and given me two gorgeous grandchildren, but she can be a bit 'up her herself' sometimes, and I'm not in the mood for a lecture on a healthy lifestyle, which is her normal pet topic.

I wash my hands, fix my smile in place and join her outside.

'Where are the kids today?'

'They're at Tumble-Tots for a couple of hours. They love it there, and I love how exhausted they are when I pick them up!'

I laugh politely and take a sip of the wine. It's a bit early in the day for me and I'm glad it's a low-alcohol-content wine.

Eleanor squints at my glass then pierces me with a *look* that could topple giants. 'You never used to drink much.'

It's an accusing statement and makes me bristle, it's none of her business if I drink or not. 'I've been known to have a little tipple now and again.'

'You had rather more than a little tipple at the anniversary party.'

Wow! 'I didn't know I was being rationed!'

'We're all worried about you, Rose.'

'What on earth for?'

'You don't seem to have been yourself lately. I've been worried that you're not well and just don't want to tell us.'

You can disguise being nosey all you want but I'd never unburden myself to you. 'I can assure you I am quite well.'

'That's what the men said, but I thought they must be wrong.'

'The men?'

'Luke, Jake and Ethan. We said we thought you were ill, they said you've never looked better.'

'You've been discussing me?' I put my glass down.

'We've just been trying to work out what's wrong.'

'Why do you think anything is wrong?'

'You and Dad seem out of sorts with each other, everyone's noticed.'

'And you think my drinking is driving him to sarcasm?'

'No, of course not, although no one's seen you drink so much before, first the party and now when we come around you always seem to have a rum and coke in your hand.'

'Oh my god!' I can't help laughing. 'So you think I'm becoming an alcoholic!'

'No, no, of course not, but increased alcohol can be an indicator that something else is going on.'

'You know what Eleanor... I never interfere when I think you're dominating Luke, so let's make a pact. I'll keep my thoughts to myself and you keep yours!' I stand up.

Eleanor is flustered and stands as well. Her face which is normally as white as chalk is now flaming red. She picks up her handbag, smooths invisible creases in her skirts and then looks at me.

'We love you, and we're worried about you. If you need to talk we're here for you.' With that she waltzes out of my sight, through the house and leaves. Leaving me in a state of regret and not liking myself much at all.

Guilt is a form of self-criticism that can beat your ego like a drummer hits a tom-tom, said psychologist Steven Berglas in Forbes – I'd read that just a few days ago in my search for how to handle what I'm going through. A single question can end up being the straw that breaks the camel's back and I think Eleanor's just done that for me. She's a lovely person, so what if she's a bit bossy and self-opinionated, she's loving and caring and I had no right to tell her I think she's domineering.

Morals and ethics are individual to our perception of life, but the brain is all-powerful. My subconscious is screaming at me, giving me that gut feeling that I need reform and I need it now before Armageddon comes screaming from the Heavens and destroys everything I hold dear.

※※ ♥ ※※

ON THE DRIVE OVER I'm determined to finish things with Joe. This has gone on too long, six weeks since the first time we got together in his flat. I'm not good at lying, any day now everything is going to burst open and leave gaping holes, and hurt, lots of hurt.

I was going to tell him straight away, I was. I practiced my speech all the way over, but I hadn't reckoned on Joe's brown eyes lighting up when he saw me. He pulls me in for a kiss as soon as I get through the door, and I give up the pretense that telling him goodbye is the only reason I'm here.

One last time… just one last time.

I try talking to him as he pulls my dress over my head. I try again when he lays me on the bed. I give up trying when his bare chest touches mine. I think he knows, every time I start to talk he kisses me to shut me up. I give up.

When we're cuddling and snuggling under the blankets, I try again, but everything I planned to say dissolves as his finger draws circles on my stomach.

'Joe…'

'Yes, baby.'

'I don't think I can do this anymore.'

'Why?'

'The urge to go back to normality is building in me. I don't like the sneaking around or the lying. I think people are getting close to learning the truth.'

'The appearance of normality you portray to everyone is not the real you.'

'But it is.'

'This is the real you, Rose. Here, with me, between the sheets.'

'There's more to life than lust.'

'This is much more than lust and you know it.'

'I don't like feeling disloyal.'

'Then chose me.'

'I can't.'

I've come to understand now, where before Joe I was ignorant – that a woman wants to yield, to offer her most precious parts to a man worthy of her womanhood. Yet tarring all those yearnings, longings and dreams of intimate connection is *reality*: discharging its dominance and creating chaos with the abandon of a child throwing paint wildly over paper. It's messy. It's very real.

'We can't control who we fall in love with, Rose. You should stop beating yourself up so much.'

'It's nonsense to say we have no control over who our hearts love, of course we do! Life is the result of the choices we make. We're here, committing adultery because we both choose to. Would not all the world be unfaithful, if they had no control and followed their whims willy-nilly? We're not children, Joe. We're grownups and we're lacking backbone.'

'Right then, return to your drab life, let the light within you – that *I* kindled – burn out. Go back to dull eyes and servant ways.'

'You're being a child.'

'At least I'm honest. Why don't you get drunk and let your true self out? *She* wants to be with me.'

My face must be downcast, for he suddenly looks contrite. 'Don't spoil what we have. This isn't something shameful, the opposite in fact. It's wonderful. I've never been so alive as I am right now. You're the only woman I've ever loved.'

'You loved Felicity.'

'Not like this, nothing like this. That's why when we split we did so as friends. We'd rushed into each other when we met, both seeking connection. We were happy for a while, and when Freddie came along we came together as a family for his sake, but we already knew we weren't going to make it as a couple. I never really loved her, not like I love you.'

He picks up my hand and brings it up to his cheek. 'Something inside me has shifted. I'm not the person I was. Now I feel whole. You've brought me to life, Rose.'

'You have to help me, Joe.'

He pulls me close, his arms like barriers of safety. 'Anything.'

'I need you to be the strong one and walk away.'

He shakes his head and removes his arms from me.

'Please Joe, please.' Tears erupt and stream like a tap.

He shakes his head again and croaks, 'Rose.'

'If you really love me you'll let me go.'

'What if you're making the wrong choice?'

'I'm not.'

'I think you are. Please choose us, Rose.'

Now it's my turn to shake my head. Grief has my throat in its grip.

'If you honestly love me like you say, then you'll help take all this pain away from me. What was pure joy has turned upside down. Now, I'm filled morning to night with the ugliness that a secret brings. It's crippling me, eating away at my soul.'

'Then tell him about us and end the lies.'

'It would kill him.'

'As you leaving will kill me.'

'No, that's not true. You're young. You'll meet someone perfect for you. You'll be fine.'

'No, I won't. I'll never love this way again.'

I get out of bed and start scrambling into my clothes. He gets out and puts his jeans on.

I run my fingers through my wavy, shoulder-length hair and hope I don't look too much like a lover who's just fallen out of bed. I pick up my bag and move to the front door. He follows. His expression is filling me with sorrow.

I move back a step towards him and grab both his hands in mine. 'I can't go on Joe. You have to let me go.'

He takes his hands from mine and wraps them around my tear-stained face. 'Tell me you love me. Just say the words once, Rose. Let me hear what my heart knows.'

I shake my head. Those three little words bind souls together. If I utter them I'll never be able to recall them. They will be in the universe forever taunting me. I can't say them. I can't give Joe hope.

He wraps his arms around me and pulls me against his chest. His heart is pounding, mine is breaking.

'I will never stop loving you. If you need me, just reach out. I'll be there, waiting.'

I should tell him not to wait, but I can't.

His arms fall to his sides.

Instantly, I experience the coldness of loss. Put them back my soul cries, while my lips remain silent.

At the door I pause.

I want to turn back and rush into his arms.

But I can't. I'm through the door and gone.

In the stairwell, I grip my chest as pain catches my breath. I stagger and reach for the wall to stay my fall. I sit on a step. With horror I realize I'm about to scream. I slap my hands over my mouth to muffle the sounds that are yanked from my soul.

I want to die.

The pain of loss is no less than that of deceit.

I imagine my husband experiencing this pain and it sobers me. Better that I should feel this than him, it is my sin after all to have wandered outside the boundaries of marriage.

I don't know how I got home. I don't remember any of the drive.

A cold shower of resolution drenches me. Thought after thought compels me to believe I have done the right thing. I look at a family portrait on the wall. A father and mother standing protectively behind their three children; their smiles telling the world that this is the life they have chosen.

As the blur of tears fades, I walk around the house with clarity. Everything appears crystal clear like my lenses have been upgraded. I'm in a world I chose, I will honor that choice and bring *all* of me back into it. My children might have grown but they need me just as much as ever. My husband might not fulfill my dreams, but he's my best friend and I will love him until the day I die. I will focus on what I have instead of longing for more. Joe will be fine. Despite his words, he will soon forget, that's the beauty of youth and all the years stretching before him. He has time to heal and to love again.

I THOUGHT THE WORST WAS OVER. I thought the pain would lessen (for both of us) and we would move forward. Time is a healer. We just need lots of time. When Joe's first text came through I had mixed emotions. Part of me sang for joy because he was still in my life, another part recoiled in horror that he was risking getting us caught.

I answered the first text. I told him he would get over me and find someone new, that there was a better woman than me out there for him. I answered the second text and told him he would be fine and that he should try and put me out of his mind… and PS., please make sure you delete your texts.

The third text made me angry. What is he up to? We'd said goodbye, we're over, finished. I sent back three words – stop texting me.

He called the house phone. Panic is now rising in me like never before.

'OK, but I can't talk to you now. I'll call you tomorrow when I'm on my own.'

He accepted that and put the phone down.

It's Thursday today. I've been in a mess ever since the phone call yesterday. I decide not to call him.

I'M BOUNCING ARTHUR ON MY KNEE when the kitchen door opens and Joe walks in. The blood drains from my head leaving my dizzy. He wouldn't… would he?

His tortoiseshell glasses, that he hardly ever wears, add wisdom and age, and intensify his stare. His expression is horribly cheerful, screaming falsehood. His eyes narrow as he glances over me and then away again without lingering.

They seem cold, not the Joe I know; they somehow threaten destructive mischief.

I have gone cold. The whole family is here. Everyone.

I want to hit him on the back of the head with the frying pan, dampen any crazy ideas that seethe under his skin. The blood in my arteries is threatening to block oxygen to my heart. The normal steady thud has become a gong of heightened speed, threatening to cut off my flow and cause my death. I hand Arthur over to my daughter.

She takes him, but she's looking at me with an odd expression.

Inside me roars. This is *not* going to happen. My family will *not* be hurt.

'You alright there, Joe?' asks my husband.

What is that look on my hubby's face?

'Actually, I've come to talk to you. Could we...'

I do the only thing I can. I faint.

I come around surrounded by worried faces. As soon as my eyes flutter open, loving hands guide me upright and back into my chair.

'Here, Mum,' says Jake passing a glass of water into my hands.

'Thanks,' I murmur, and as I take a sip I search for Joe. He's gone, well not in the kitchen anyway.

'What happened, love? Should I call an ambulance?'

He's still calling me love, so I assume Joe's not said his piece. 'No, no. I'm fine. I just don't think I've eaten today.'

A flurry of worried comments rain down on me. My heart rate has slowed and I'm beginning to feel normal again, and then Joe returns from the hallway. Where has he been? Had he been on his way out? Why did he stop?

We lock eyes, Joe and I. The rest of the people in the kitchen fade into a nondescript blur of color and sound. We say a thousand things to each other without saying a single word. His pallor is pale, wan even and I know he was scared for me. His pain, in not being able to touch me and send everyone else away, flies with arrow precision and pierces my determined armor.

I should be strong, I should.

Why do I feel so weak?

Only I notice Joe turn around and leave. I've won this battle, but I know I'm losing the war. I can't find the strength to do what needs to be done. I know I will have to persuade Joe to be the strong one, but how?

Swan-Song

HIS TEXT READS... *One last time or I'll tell everyone.*

His blackmail should make me angry, but it just makes me sad. Of course I go to see him, one last Saturday morning. I forgive the threat, I know he's hurting. I will try and make him understand. I will try and ease his pain.

We don't talk when I arrive, he looks sheepish, and so he should. But then my love for him pours out of me. Seeing his heartache is almost too much to bear. I need to do everything I can to lessen the grief he's going through. First, I will offer my body for what must be the last time, and then I will reach out to his mind.

I see his surprise when I start to undress. I guess he was expecting an argument. I take his hand and pull him to the bed. I kiss his body, each and every one of them a goodbye to his flesh. When we make love, it's tender and far too sad. I have a feeling I'm going to be haunted by this last time forever.

'I love you.'

What can I say? How can I answer? All our secret rendezvous haven't been just about sex... not all the time. We've grown into each other. We fit snugly. We know our bodies. When we're not in the throes of passion he holds me close, making me feel special and desired. That's heady stuff. We are one, for what good is a song without a singer, or a poem without a reader?

But love? I can't give him that. I need to set him free. I'm holding my breath for what comes next.

'Leave him.'

'Joe!'

'Leave him, move in with me.'

'No!' I push back the covers, but before I can escape the inevitable crossfire of words, Joe pins me down and straddles me. Gripping my wrists he holds my arms down above my head.

'Why not?'

'There's not enough time to give you all the reasons.'

'Then just give me the good ones, and for God's sake don't mention age.'

It's pointless to blurt out the obvious. I struggle in his grip, he just stares at me.

'Come on Rose; tell me why we shouldn't be happy.'

Just then the song switches. Joe jumps up, standing on the bed, from the second note he knew what song was coming on. He sings it to me, standing there like a Greek god, his fine physique bouncing on the mattress.

I laugh, I can't help myself, but it's cheerless. 'You're nuts.'

He carries on singing, when he gets to this bit he drops to his knees and sings right in front of me…

And who's gonna kiss you when I'm gone

Oh, I'm gonna love you now, like it's all I have

(John Legend, Love me Now 2016)

His breath escapes at the end of the line of the song. His chest is rising and falling rapidly. There are tears in his eyes.

'I can't.'

'Why?'

God but the lyrics are crushing me…

Who's going to love me when it's over?

I feel the same. No one will ever love me like Joe does.

'Don't cry.' Joe drops down next to me and pulls my head into his chest. I soak his skin with heart-wrenching sobs.

Another love song comes on. 'Please turn it off.'

He scrambles for the control and switches the music off. Silence covers our naked flesh with a terrible countdown. It's not comfortable, it's pregnant with anticipation. His of hope, mine of dread and a creeping sense of doom.

'This is just a dream,' I whisper.

'No it's not.' He pushes me away from him so we can look at each other.

'I love you and I know you love me. Don't even try to deny it, because I *know.*'

'But love – this type of love – isn't enough.'

'What do you mean this type of love?'

'Our love is selfish.'

He jumps out of bed. For a moment he just stares at me with his hands pushed through his hair, and then he starts walking up and down.

'For goodness' sake, if you're going to pace like that, please put on a pair of shorts or something. Wagging your weapon in front of me like that isn't going to make me change my mind.' No matter how much I love it!

He pulls boxers on. I sit up and drag the sheet up under my armpits.

'I love you,' Joe repeats.

As much as I want to tell him I love him, I can't. I don't want to build up his hopes.

'Love isn't enough.'

'What? I can't provide you with a big detached house so you're giving up on us!'

I sigh, and for a brief moment close my eyes.

'There are more things to life, and I don't mean possessions – they mean nothing to me – I mean relationships. I love my husband for a start.'

'Yeah right, but he doesn't make you feel like I do.' His answer is cocky, but also very self-assured.

'What makes you think that?'

'Have you looked in the mirror lately?'

That wasn't the answer I was expecting. My crinkles multiply as I squint at him.

'Oh my god, don't tell me you can't see!'

'See what?'

He shakes his head in wonder. 'Honestly, it's amazing how everyone hasn't guessed you're having an affair... with a young, sexy stud!' He waggles his eyebrows at me and I can't help but smile, though there's no joy in it.

'You're glowing Rose, and you have been since our first kiss in your kitchen. Your eyes haven't stopped sparkling and you're always laughing. You're happy and it's damn-right obvious.'

The trouble is... I think everyone *has* noticed.

He sits down on the bed next to me and takes my hand. 'These last six weeks you've become another woman. Anyone with half a brain can see you're in love.'

I pull my hand out of his. 'They'll assume I love my husband.'

'And who will *he* assume you're in love with?'

Panic flutters across my skin. Is it possible my husband has guessed something's going on? Is that why he's been so sharp lately? Has he seen this change in me, and is that why he's been particularly short-tempered? Oh no, no, no. This is terrible. Does he know about Joe?

I start fighting with the covers. I need to get dressed. I need to go home. I stumble out of bed and start gathering my clothes.

Joe gets up and stands in front of the door. He folds his arms. 'You're not going anywhere until we finish this conversation.'

'I've got to get home.' My hands are shaking as I grapple with my blouse buttons.

Joe comes over and starts doing them up for me, with agonizing slowness. 'I want to marry you, Rose.'

The room spins.

'I got you. Sit down.' He guides me back to the bed where we perch on the edge.

When my panic-panting slows, I state, 'I'm already married.'

'Divorce is easy these days.'

'Not for people who love each other!' Shrill-panic puts my voice on screech level. 'I can't divorce him!'

'You can.'

'No. No. No.'

'I'll never leave you alone. I'll bombard you with passion until you're too weak to resist.' His tone is playful, half-joking – but only half.

'You said one last time, I don't think you're a liar, keep your word Joe. I love my husband. I'm not going to leave him.'

'You will.'

'I WON'T!' I get up and finish dressing. 'This is *over*. I don't want to see you again, Joe.'

Joe stands and wraps his arms around my waist, nuzzling my neck with his chin. 'Look, I've surprised you. I'll give you time to think about it.'

'I don't need time. I'm telling you now, I'm *never* getting divorced.' I stride from the bedroom into the hallway. As I'm reaching for the front door, Joe says, 'So you're going to choose *him* over me?' He sounds incredulous, oh, the arrogance of youth!

I turn around and pin him with a stare that only mothers can master. 'I'm not choosing him over *you*. I'm choosing my family over *me*!'

'If you don't tell him, I will.'

'Joe! You can't!'

'I want you to be happy.'

'I am happy, you idiot. Joe, don't do anything stupid… please. If you do I will *never* speak to you again as long as I live, so you will have lost me anyway. Only now you will have also made a lot of people unhappy. Trust me Joe; I don't ever go back on *my* word!'

Before he can respond I leave.

Panic is turning into dread and my innards are freezing, like they've been taken out of my body and dumped across the ice in the Antarctic.

What have I done?

Why do I feel like screaming?

I'm shaking as I get in the car.

Have I risked everything just to feel young again?

Am I really such an idiot?

What if Joe goes ahead with his threat and tells my husband we've been having an affair? If Harvey asked me outright I couldn't lie. I'd have to admit it. Then what?

I pound the steering wheel.

'Stupid. Stupid. Stupid, old woman!'

I've got to get home.

The drive is a blur.

I leave the keys in the front door.

Salmon. We're having steamed salmon for dinner. I take the fish and vegetables out of the fridge.

Shower! Oh for goodness' sake. The smell!

I drop the knife on the chopping board and rush up the stairs, taking my clothes off as I run. I throw them into the washing basket and dive into the shower.

Manic scrubbing turns my skin red. I turn up the heat as high as it will go, almost scalding my flesh.

I scrub between my legs. I'll never smell like this again as long as I live. Sobs bend me double.

I sink to my knees. The water crashes against my back.

'Joe,' I wail. 'Joe I love you, I love you. I love you.'

Time passes.

Water cleanses.

My tears fade.

I need to get out of here. I need to wash my clothes, and to throw away my attempt at sexy underwear – before my husband sees them! I need to start dinner.

I'm running out of time.

Yet here is the problem with having an immortal spirit encased in a *very* mortal body.

My knees have gone. The grab rail my clever, kind, thoughtful Harvey put in is just out of reach. I switch off the shower.

'Please God, please help me up.'

I try one way and then another. I push. I try to reach the rail. Frustration causes the tears that had subsided to return.

'Rose, are you in there?'

Oh no!

I don't want to answer. I want to be invisible. Weak, so weak. 'I need your help, love.'

The bathroom door opens and in walks my handsome husband, his face full of love and concern.

I weep.

He rushes over and opens the shower door and bends down. 'Here, wrap your arms around me.'

I'm drowning, expressed with deafening sobs.

'Oh love, it's alright, I've got you.'

And he does. Slowly, slowly, my treacherous curse-worthy knees allow my legs to unfold and my tender, kind, sweet Harvey helps me to stand up.

After wrapping a robe around me, he helps me over to the bed where I sit on the edge. He pulls over my dresser stool and sits in front of me. Without saying anything he takes the towel that was over his shoulder and starts rubbing my hair dry. Would Joe care for me like this?

The tears just won't stop.

'Come on love, you're OK now.'

The lump in my throat turns my words into croaks. 'Getting old is shit.'

He chuckles. 'Yes, but at least we're getting old together.'

'Your body's not falling apart like mine.'

'Maybe not, but isn't that a good thing? I mean how would I look after you if I was?'

I want to smile, but I can't manage it. Instead, I take his hand and bring it to my lips to place a gentle kiss on it. 'Thank you,' I whisper.

'Anytime.'

I'm a horrible person.

'I'll go and start dinner. I see you've got salmon out.'

I nod.

'Do you have your tablets here?'

I nod again.

He smiles. 'Good, just come down when you're ready.'

Water's dripping down my back.

The alarm clock ticks with shattering loudness.

I have it all: a husband who loves me, children, grandchildren, a beautiful home, lots of friends, and a comfortable life. So why do I want the one thing that will take all of this away from me?

I drop the robe and walk naked over to the full-length mirror. My uncombed grey hair, lovingly tousled by my husband is standing out in all directions. My eyes are dull with large dark circles under them. My face is full of red blotches. My boobs and tummy (from recent weight loss) are sagging. I am dull. No sparkle. No laughing eyes. No more need be said to describe my sorrowful reflection. I am sorry that age has become such an issue for me, but I'm saddened even more that without Joe life may slip away from me altogether.

Sad, I turn away and get myself dressed.

Clothes – the camouflage of my mortal flesh.

I practice the smile I will give my husband when I get downstairs.

Smiles – the camouflage of my eternal soul.

Joe peeked beneath my camouflage and saw me. He looked into my soul and saw my sorrow, my loneliness, my desperate need to *be* a woman. Having seen me, he has gingerly wrapped his mantle of protectiveness around me.

His love flamed, and so did mine.

As my womanhood has awakened, my love for this young man has consumed me. He fulfills me.

I am desired.

Is it the way he makes me feel, that makes me love him? I don't honestly know. But I'm in love with him, will always be in love with him.

I'm so damn thankful.

I'm not ugly after all. Some men do find me attractive.

Just not my husband.

Like I told Joe, there are many types of love. My husband is my best friend; we laughingly say we're soul mates. We're comfortable together; know each other inside out – almost. I love him.

I love my kids and my grandkids, my family and my friends. I love our home, especially the garden. I love going to church. I love reading and writing. I love cooking, and I love giving gifts that make people smile.

All these things I love, but I'm *in* love with Joe.

He awoke my soul.

He made me feel young, God bless him for that!

He flooded me with indescribable joy.

In another world…

But I live here, this is my life.

I wrap my arms around my body and close my eyes.

Instantly, my insides contract as thoughts of Joe flood my mind.

I open them again. No more tears. No more dreams. I cross the room and stare out of the window into our beloved garden. Looking out I recall the first time Joe wrapped his arms around me, and I'd realized that I missed sex. You see Harvey and I may be close, and we definitely love each other, but the last time he touched me sensually was on our seventh wedding anniversary, thirty-three years ago.

Since then nothing has brought us as close as only making love can do.

Our love is strong, or how would we still be together?

But the connection that comes when two people offer their bodies to one another brings a whole other thing, a bond I'd thought I didn't mind living without.

Joe reminded me about that bond when he wrapped his arms around me. Later, when his body covered mine, he reminded me that there is another way to love. A giving of self that involves mind, soul *and* body.

CHRISTMAS ALWAYS BRINGS ME such joy. I love everything about it; it's fair to say I'm one of Christmas's biggest fans. This year, however, a veil lays over my every smile.

I know I've made the right choice, but that doesn't stop me thinking about Joe every day. I miss him, painfully so. Christmas is a time when he and Freddie would have spent a great deal of time at our house. He's going to take Freddie to Scotland this year, so Jake tells us. I'm sad that we can't be as we were before.

Three days before Christmas is a Saturday, Harvey is of course at the golf club spending more time in the 19th hole than on the green. Everyone is coming to us for dinner on Christmas day, so I have plenty to keep me busy. I'm in the process of making a gingerbread house when I hear the letterbox rattle followed by a light thud.

I wipe my icing-sugar covered hands on my apron and go to the door. It's a hand-delivered card. I pick it up and stare at it as I go back to the kitchen. Half way back I stop. It suddenly dawns on me that I recognize the writing. The card is from Joe. I rush back to the door and yank it open and run into the driveway. There's no one around.

'Oh Joe, you could have said hello.' Tears sting behind my eyes as I head back inside. From the thickness of the envelope I know there is something more inside than just a card. The card simply says 'To the clan, wishing you all a very merry Christmas, see you in the new year, love Joe and Freddie.' But inside the card is a piece of paper folded in half, on the outside it simply says 'Rose.' There is also something wrapped up in tissue. He's delivered it on a day he knew I would be by myself, a day that used to be ours.

I go into the front room and sit down. As I open the page my hands are trembling.

My dearest Rose,

And you are, you know, mine. I have this understanding in my chest that neither of us will ever be complete. We are destined to live with something missing in our lives.

But I'm not writing to be melancholy or to make you feel bad, I'm writing to say thank you. Thank you for giving yourself to me the way you did, so openly and honestly. You warmed my heart and filled me with happiness.

I want you to know that for a while I must stay away from you because I don't trust what I would do if I saw you right now, but I hope that one day I will be man enough to seek your friendship once again. I miss my second home. I miss your smile.

You know why men go to war Rose? It's to protect the ones they love. My battle is only with myself, but it's a battle I will fight every day to ensure I stay away from you so that you can live in peace.

I love you Rose, now and forever.

Joe x

Though I'm sobbing I'm happy, for now I know that he will, one day, return into our lives, for the thought of not knowing how he is doing has been killing me. Now I know he'll be alright, and one day he'll come back into our lives.

When the crying stops and I can see clearly again, I open the tissue, I have butterflies in my stomach.

Tears roll again; I have no idea where all the water comes from! The bracelet I fell in love with in Fira is in my hands.

Life after Love

How Do I Love Thee? (Sonnet 43) Elizabeth Barrett Browning
1806-1861 (In public domain)

How do I love thee? Let me count the ways.
I love thee to the depth and breadth and height
My soul can reach, when feeling out of sight
For the ends of being and ideal grace.
I love thee to the level of every day's
Most quiet need, by sun and candle-light.
I love thee freely, as men strive for right.
I love thee purely, as they turn from praise.
I love thee with the passion put to use
In my old griefs, and with my childhood's faith.
I love thee with a love I seemed to lose
With my lost saints. I love thee with the breath,
Smiles, tears, of all my life; and, if God choose,
I shall but love thee better after death.

The Following Year

YOU CAN'T ALWAYS GUARANTEE the weather in England even in July. Today, however, is glorious. As people arrive for my birthday gathering they automatically walk around the side of the house and enter through the side gate. I love that our family and friends know us so well as to know we're in the garden, and are comfortable enough to simply walk in.

They gather around, our band of loved and dear ones – all ages and personalities.

Harvey has the music blasting, everyone is talking loud to compensate. I flap my hands at him; he understands, pulls a moaning face but takes the remote out of his pocket and turns it down... slightly, before walking away hand in hand with our grandson.

Daphne nudges me. 'Whatever happened to Joe?'

I sip my drink and hope someone else will answer.

Melody comes to my rescue. 'I think I heard that he's met someone and has moved to Cornwall to live with her.'

'Is that right?' says Daphne, like it's the biggest piece of news she's ever heard. 'Has he married again?'

Melody shrugs. 'No, I don't think so.'

She's partly right. I know he hasn't moved away, but he does have a new girlfriend, and for that I am very grateful. He didn't notice me, but I saw Joe with her at the shops last week. He looked happy. Knowing he has been able to move on fills my heart with thankfulness and relief. I have been so worried about him.

Just then Jake comes by. Daphne grabs his elbow. 'Hey Jake, is Joe in Cornwall?'

'Nah, he goes there a lot, met some girl, but Freddie is here so he'll never move away.'

'How's he doing?' asks Daphne.

I'm holding my breath. I need to know he's OK.

'He's alright. After some chick broke his heart I wasn't sure he was going to be, but he seems to be pulling through now. This new girl helps, which is good. She's a single mum and they have a lot in common.'

'What's her name?' asks Melody.

'Jeanette. She's a nurse and seems like a lovely person. She makes Joe laugh all the time, so you gotta love that about her.'

'Oh that's lovely. Joe is such a nice young lad, I'm glad he's met someone,' says Daphne.

I drink to dispel the lump in my throat. I'm glad too. So, so, glad.

'Nana, Nana.'

Oh thank God! I put my drink down and brace for the voracious hug that's about to come.

'Nana!' Little arms grab my leg tightly. I think my heart's melting.

Please don't tell my kids, but... I think the love of a grandchild is probably the best kind of love there is.

'Nana come and play.' Chloe grabs my hand and starts pulling me away.

'Duty calls,' I laugh to my friends.

I jog over to the sandpit, where two of our grandsons are already building a castle.

My husband looks up from the grass, where he lies with our youngest grandchild Arthur, who's climbing all over him. He is the sweetest, kindest, tenderhearted grandparent any child could want.

He winks at me. 'Come on, time to play.'

I bend with ease, the beauty of two new knees. I thank God for my titanium implants and for the joy of being able to play with my grandchildren. I also thank him for my husband who loves me very much, in his own special way. He'd paid for my knees to be done privately. The NHS waiting list, he said, is a crying shame.

I've never told anyone of my affair, just like I've never told anyone that I think my husband is gay. Both things are private, both are bitterly painful. For years I convinced myself it was because I was ugly and fat that my husband didn't touch me. I hated myself. I'd look in the mirror and cry and go straight to the freezer for some ice cream to console myself. When I understood that Joe fancied me it restored something in me and confirmed that I am attractive, I guess that's why I lost my head so much.

Letting go of Joe was the hardest thing I've ever done in my life. I still question whether I made the right decision sometimes. I confess I think of him every single day. I'm glad to hear that he is happy.

I'm grateful to him for our six weeks of passion. For awakening the flame of youth inside me; it might not be fanned into life by his touch anymore but I'm quietly delighted it has never fully faded.

I've purchased toys, and now when my husband plays golf, I play by myself. In those moments, alone, I picture Joe and recall memories of him. They create havoc with my body. The memory with the most impact is the one when he first touched me, that innocent grip that melted me. And in melting I released something that only Joe had perceived... the fact that I wanted an intimate relationship.

I think he'd smile if he knew he was still giving me pleasure.

Harvey Delaney had been harboring a dread for years that he wouldn't be enough for his Rose. That she would leave him one day had seemed a fait accompli. When he'd figured out that she was having an affair with Joe, he'd sunk into dreaded acceptance and waited with bated breath for her to approach him.

Day after day had slipped by and his fixed smile had become rigid as he hid his fear and utter panic. How had she not seen? Throughout the six weeks he'd held his breath and willed her, even prayed, that she would choose him. When she packed to go on holiday, he'd thought she might never return.

He would have let her go if that had been what she wanted. She deserved to be happy. He'd seen life spring into her eyes and her step; he'd heard her giggles and increased merriment in her singing. He was no fool. He knew she'd fallen in love.

He hated himself for spying on her, in her own way (despite her affair) she is so innocent, it would never occur to her that he'd put a 'find my phone' in her mobile, and the tracker revealed her every move: when she drove to Joe's house instead of the pictures, when she went to Wales, when she went to the reservoir. He'd hated himself and had been full of his own guilt for spying on her; he'd just not been able to help himself. He knew he should have confronted her about it, but fear that she would choose Joe meant he could never verbalize the panic and anger that mingled inside him.

The day the affair ended had been obvious to him. The day he'd found her sobbing in the shower. The light in her eyes had dimmed, her shoulders slumped, her step heavy. Her tears had rolled, not for the ineffectiveness of her knees, but for her loss. His heart had sung with joy! He'd tried very hard not to drown her in gifts of thankfulness, lest she cotton on to his relief, but he had splashed the cash, he just couldn't help himself.

From the day he had moved into a separate bedroom, he knew he risked losing her. She was a vibrant, passionate woman; he knew he didn't deserve her, being unable to meet her needs as he was. Still, they'd always been close and talked about everything – except their secret desires. He'd been a fool to even consider the fact she might not mind, that somehow although all women enjoyed bedroom activities – his wife should be the one exception. How stupid. How delusional. And yet he had hoped, and over the years (he can now clearly see), he'd come to believe he was safe. He wanted to talk to her about Joe, but that might encourage her to question his desires, and that was somewhere he didn't want to go.

So they kept silent about their secrets, harboring their inner turmoils so as not to let them out and destroy their intricate relationship. A silent pact made between their souls to lessen the extent of the pain of betrayal.

He still went to golf on the weekends and still enjoyed his Friday night steaks. But as to the rest of the week he'd become open to change. He accepted her invitations to go to the cinema, or to go walking. They continued with their morning crossword, but he moved his chair a little closer, and smiled from his heart as they talked. He never wanted to take her for granted again, and he wanted her to know that she was his everything.

Their love for each other had changed; the result of that change was a deeper connection. They were grateful to have each other and from that gratitude stemmed a deeper commitment to ensuring each other's happiness.

THE MONA LISA needs to be seen only once for the impression of its exquisiteness to remain forever planted in your soul. Once imprinted in the mind its beauty feeds the soul eternally if you draw upon its memory.

Now the affair is over, I'm surprisingly free from guilt. Nor do I carry resentment that my husband is apathetic towards my womanly needs. He is what he is and I am what I am, and thankfully we love each other despite that. I believe that love *beyond* the sheets is a far better thing. Friendship, mutual respect and consideration, all these fire a furnace that never dims, this love is eternal, and for that my heart overflows with gratitude.

My husband loves me without makeup or fancy clothes; in fact he cuddles me more when I'm in my pajamas than a bodacious dress. He doesn't mind that age is adding lines to my face and inches to my waist. He doesn't demand my full attention, but glows when I listen and chip in with my penny's worth. We're comfortable together, yes… like a pair of old slippers!

The wobble – my stray into infidelity – was fleeting, a passing tempest in my otherwise faithful marriage. I treasure the memories of my time with Joe, like something precious.

I'm lassoed to the nostalgia of a forbidden love, though I'm content with the choices I made and at peace with the present. Our frolicking with a daring and intense love, made us dance upon danger. Our beguiling affair began a tango of choice between us that tore at the core of our essence. We're not bad people, Joe and I. We were but mere moths to the flame of desire. Fun and mischief pulled me from my nest of comfort and propriety, love saw me safely returned.

The memory of those six weeks with Joe will remain my treasured secret until the day I die. But if I were to believe in reincarnation, then I would ask the universe to allow me and Joe to come together again, in a time when we would be free to choose one another. In *that* life, we would dance and dance and dance, and sing, and his arms would wrap around my waist and remind me that I *am* an attractive woman after all.

Thank you so much for reading Rose and Joe's story, I hope you enjoyed their short romance.

If you have time to pop a review onto Amazon I would really appreciate it, reader's words of encouragement mean the world to me.

Sincerely, Angelina

Author Information

If you'd like to read other books by me, you can find them here:

https://www.amazon.com/stores/Angelina-Amoss/author/B0BH4KPYX5

If you enjoyed this book you might also enjoy my other book under my pen name Nancy Orchard:

Contemporary Romance

https://www.amazon.com/dp/B06XD1PT7T